10 GREAT DATES

BEFORE YOU SAY "I DO"

Other Resources from David and Claudia Arp

Books

10 Great Dates to Energize Your Marriage
52 Dates for You and Your Mate
Answering the 8 Cries of the Spirited Child
Empty Nesting
Family Moments
Love Life for Parents
Marriage Moments
Quiet Whispers from God's Heart for Couples
The Second Half of Marriage
Suddenly They're 13!

Video Curriculum

10 Great Dates to Energize Your Marriage
PEP Groups for Parents
The Second Half of Marriage

10 GREAT DATES
BEFORE YOU SAY "I DO"

David & Claudia Arp
and
Curt & Natelle Brown

ZONDERVAN®

ZONDERVAN.com/
AUTHORTRACKER
follow your favorite authors

ZONDERVAN

10 *Great Dates Before You Say "I Do"*
Copyright © 2003 by David and Claudia Arp and Curt and Natelle Brown

Requests for information should be addressed to:

Zondervan, *Grand Rapids, Michigan* 49530

Library of Congress Cataloging-in-Publication Data
10 great dates before you say "I do" / David and Claudia Arp and Curt and Natelle Brown.
   p. cm.
   Includes bibliographical references.
   ISBN 978-0-310-24732-6
   1. Dating (Social customs). 2. Mate selection. 3. Mate selection—Religious aspects—Christianity. I.
Title: Ten great dates before you say "I do". II. Arp, Dave.
   HQ801 .A12 2003
   646.7'7—dc21

   2002014056

The names and identifying details of the individuals in the stories within have been changed to protect their privacy.

Published in association with the literary agency of Alive Communications, Inc., 7680 Goddard Street, Suite 200, Colorado Springs, CO 80920. www.alivecommunications.com

Interior design by Sherri L. Hoffman

Printed in the United States of America

13 14 • 32 31 30 29 28 27 26 25 24 23 22 21 20 19 18 17 16 15

To our son, Courtney, and our daughter, Carissa
May you each meet and marry the love of your life, and may you
enjoy these 10 great dates before you say "I do"

Curt and Natelle

To all those who mentor and work with seriously
dating and engaged couples
May this resource complement the important role you play in
pre-marriage education

Dave and Claudia

Contents

Acknowledgments

We are deeply indebted to the many people who contributed to this project and gratefully acknowledge the contributions of the following people:

- All the seriously dating, engaged, and newlywed couples whom we have had the privilege to mentor and coach and to all the couples who tested these 10 great dates;
- All the many couples who have participated in our Marriage Alive seminars over the years and who have shared with us your struggles and success stories;
- Those who have pioneered pre-marriage education and on whose shoulders we stand including David Olson, Les and Leslie Parrott, David and Vera Mace, Norm Wright, Emily and Dennis Lowe, and our friends at PREP, including Scott Stanley, Howard Markman, Susan Blumberg and Natalie Jenkins. We especially thank Barbara Markey and Mike and Harriet McManus for your helpful suggestions in preparing this manuscript and to Dianne Sollee for all you have done and are doing to encourage pre-marriage and marriage education;
- The many other researchers and authors from whom we quoted, for your sound work that gives a solid base for the cause of pre-marriage education;
- Our Zondervan team who have believed and supported us over the years, for your encouragement and excitement about this new resource. We especially thank our publisher, Scott Bolinder, our editors, Sandy Vander Zicht and Angela Scheff, and our marketing team, John Topliff, Greg Stielstra, and Cindy Wilcox, for helping to get the word out, and to Curt Diepenhorst for making the cover so appealing. We also thank author relations experts, Joyce Ondersma and Jackie Aldridge, for taking such good care of us;
- Our literary agent, Greg Johnson of Alive Communications, for being our advocate, and encouraging us along the way.

Welcome to Your 10 Great Dates

Welcome to your own personal 10 Great Dates! We're glad you are taking the time to get to know each other better. We hope you will relax and enjoy focusing on the present while preparing for the future. Whether you are engaged or seriously considering marriage, you'll have the opportunity to see your relationship more clearly, to pay attention to each other, and to laugh and affirm one another.

Our dates have been crafted to help seriously dating and engaged couples evaluate their relationships and decide if they want to take the next step. If you have already made the commitment to marry, these dates will help you confirm that you are indeed ready for marriage and you can move ahead with confidence that marriage is *your* next best step! And as you are confirming your commitment, don't forget to have some fun along the way.

Each date will help you concentrate on a specific skill needed to build a successful marriage. You will learn how to communicate better and handle the differences we promise will appear!

Our dates are based on more than two decades of experience and practical input from couples who have participated in our Marriage Alive seminars and *10 Great Dates* programs as well as input from many engaged couples. Our dates are also based on the sage advice from marital researchers and those who have designed helpful marital inventories and pre-marriage preparation programs. You can trust each date to be a faithful guide in enriching your relationship now and in the years ahead.

While you are dating, we hope you are also taking advantage of other resources to help you prepare for marriage. Perhaps you have already signed up for a premarital education class. If not, please take advantage of one of the excellent premarital inventories like PREPARE and FOCCUS[1] that will help you assess your strengths and weaknesses. Conferences, video programs, and books about preparing for marriage (like this one) can give valuable insights (see Appendix, page 139). You may also want to consider premarital counseling and mentoring opportunities.

If you don't already have a mentor couple, find one! Mike and Harriet McManus, cofounders of Marriage Savers, believe a key to a successful marriage is meeting with a qualified and trained mentor couple for several months before the wedding. The mentor couple should typically have been married for over fifteen years and can share the realities of marriage from their own personal experience. Mentor couples don't claim to have perfect marriages, but they can be a valuable resource of marital wisdom, as well as helping you avoid and survive some of the pitfalls they encountered.[2] Now let us introduce you to your *10 Great Dates* dating guides.

MEET YOUR DATING GUIDES

We, Dave and Claudia and Curt and Natelle, will be your personal dating guides. We have been dating for years and between us have logged over thirty years' experience working with couples—both engaged and married.

We, Claudia and Dave, coined the phrase, "Fun in marriage is serious business." Dating is one way to keep the fun factor alive before and after you say "I do." Over the last twenty-five years, thousands have attended our Marriage Alive seminar, which we lead both in the United States and in Europe. In addition, over 100,000 couples have used our dating resources to energize their relationships.

We, Natelle and Curt, bring fresh experiences from mentoring engaged couples and leading seminars. Several years ago, Natelle completed a master's degree in Marriage and Family Therapy, and Curt sold his computer business to his partner. Together we joined the staff of Marriage Alive. We love working with seriously dating and engaged couples. That's why we are excited about helping you get the most out of your great dates.

Sprinkled through the following pages are our own personal experiences as well as stories from many couples with whom we have worked who, just like you, want to build a loving, lasting marriage. (Names and circumstances have been altered to protect their privacy.)

If you want to know more about us, refer to the About the Authors page in the back of the book. We want to share with you our passion for helping you prepare for your future marriage so that it will be all that you dream and hope for. Our prayer for you is that your marriage will be a marriage after God's own heart. Ready? Let's get started!

GET READY FOR 10 GREAT DATES

Now is the time to escape from the daily cares and routine. We encourage you to get ready for ten fantastic dating experiences based on the following dating themes.

Date One: Sharing Hopes, Dreams, and Expectations

Date One will help you look at your expectations and consider which ones are realistic. Remembering together favorite dates in the past and looking at your relationship as it is right now will help you cast a vision of what you want your relationship to be like in the future.

Date Two: Appreciating Your Differences

Date Two is designed to help you better understand the ways you are alike and the ways you are different. Appreciating your differences is foundational to building a strong marriage partnership, so on this date you will have the opportunity to consider how you can complement each other in the ways you are different.

Date Three: Communicating and Connecting

Communication may seem easy now, but couples in all ages and stages of marriage say communication is one of the top three issues in their marriage. This date offers the opportunity to learn communication skills that have been tested and proven to help couples stay connected with each other after marriage.

Date Four: Solving Problems as a Couple

Date Four is crafted to help you learn ways to resolve honest conflict by working through problems together. You may think a date on problem solving is not as exciting as some of the others, but everyone needs to know how to process anger so it builds the relationship instead of tearing it down.

Date Five: Managing Your Money

Most newly married couples struggle on some level with finances. Date Five is designed to help you talk about this delicate subject before you say "I do." Will you combine your income, or do you plan to keep your finances separate? This is a great time to talk about your expectations and consider how you might want to handle your finances after marriage.

Date Six: Leaving and Cleaving

How much do you know about each other's growing-up years? Date Six will help you better understand your families of origin and your expectations for future involvement with your families. And how will your friendships—both individual and mutual—affect your marriage? The most enjoyable part of this date may be exploring how you can keep your own friendship strong and fun quotient high.

Date Seven: Celebrating Intimacy, Love, and Romance

Many couples are concerned that romance may die after they say "I do." This doesn't have to happen. Date Seven will help you define what intimacy, love, and romance mean to you. You will have the opportunity to talk about the facets of a love life and how to get your differing desires and expectations in sync.

Date Eight: Realizing Roles and Planning for Family

This date is designed to help you talk candidly about your expectations concerning roles in marriage and how you want to divide and share chores and life tasks. You will also have the opportunity to talk about family planning and, if applicable, how bringing children into the marriage will affect your relationship.

Date Nine: Developing Spiritual Intimacy

The purpose of this date is to share together where you are on your spiritual quest and to look at ways to develop spiritual intimacy. Maybe one grew up in a Christian home and the other is just beginning the spiritual journey. This date will give you the opportunity to talk about your spiritual expectations—will you pray together and have shared devotions? Will you attend the same church and participate in church activities? How would you like to reach out and together serve others?

Date Ten: Choosing an Intentional Marriage

This last date is designed to be a time of reconfirming your commitment to each other, or if you're seriously dating, to perhaps make some decisions about where you want your relationship to go. You will have the opportunity to consider what marriage involvement style will work best for you. Setting marriage goals can help you turn your desires and dreams for your marriage into reality.

YOUR PERSONAL DATING GUIDE

The second part of the book is your own personal Dating Guide. We've taken care of the details so you can concentrate on each other. You will find a pre-date guide with suggestions for how to prepare for each date, ideas for where to go and how to approach each date, and how to benefit from the exercises.

While it is desirable for both of you to read the corresponding chapter before the date and fill out the exercise, we realize sometimes this just won't happen. So with each Dating Guide we have included a brief chapter summary.

While *10 Great Dates* is designed to help one couple at a time, it is also appropriate to use for small group studies. If you know you need the pressure of being committed to others, recruit other engaged or seriously dating couples and go through *10 Great Dates* together.

What Will Be the Dating Format?

How do these *10 Great Dates* work? It's quite simple. First, read the corresponding chapter before each date. If only one reads the chapter, that person can take the lead in planning the date and guiding the conversation.

Second, go on your date. In a relaxed atmosphere away from interruptions, you will have the opportunity to talk through the short exercises that will help you fine-tune a specific skill to enhance your relationship. The practical application during the date in an atmosphere of fun is the secret of having great dates!

The difference between reading a book and having your relationship enriched is your involvement. Statistics suggest that it takes three weeks to start a good habit or to break a bad one, and six weeks to feel good about either. We suggest ten weeks of dates to strengthen your relationship. Plus we are hoping your date night will be a habit you will take into your marriage. You can reap the benefits of your great dates long past these initial ten.

LAUNCHING YOUR GREAT DATES

The following steps will help you begin your dating experience on a positive note:

1. Agree to go on all ten dates. It really doesn't matter who found the book or whose idea it was. Maybe your mentors gave you this book, or it was recommended in your marriage preparation class or when you took a premarital inventory. Maybe you aren't engaged yet, but you found this book in a bookstore or on the Internet. Whatever your situation, agreeing to go on ten dates will help you take a closer look at your relationship.

2. Schedule your dates and write them in your calendar.

3. Clear your schedule.

4. Plan for possible interruptions. Despite the best planning, you may have to change your plans. When this happens, reschedule your date for the same week and persevere. Hang in there, and value your time together. Don't let wedding preparation crowd out time for dating and focusing on each other!

5. Anticipate each date. Let the other know you are looking forward to being together. Be clever. Send notes and give hints that you expect a great date.

6. Before the date, read through the chapter and note key topics to discuss. If you take time to complete the short exercise before the date, you will have more time for intimate conversations. But you can also do the exercise on the date.
7. Follow our simple guide for each date, and stay on topic. Don't use date time to deal with other issues and problems.
8. Stay positive! It is hard to be negative when you are holding hands.
9. Get started! The key to building a successful marriage is taking the time to work on the relationship, and the more work you do before the wedding, the better.

Make a Commitment

Our *10 Great Dates* will only make a difference if you do them. Like most anything worthwhile, preparing for marriage takes time. Good intentions aren't enough. A written commitment can help carry you through. Use the commitment form that follows to record your promise to each other.

You will be glad you took the time to encourage, build up, and appreciate one another. Remember, yesterday is past, and tomorrow is in the future. Today is the only gift of time you've been given; that's why it is called "the present." So, during this special time in your life, give each other the present of *10 Great Dates!*

MAKING A COMMITMENT

I agree to invest time in building our relationship through going on 10 Great Dates.

Officially Signed:
His signature_____
Her signature _____
Date _____
Our first date is scheduled for _____

Part One

10 Great Dates

Date One

Sharing Hopes, Dreams, and Expectations

"For I know the plans I have for you," declares the Lord, "plans to prosper you and not to harm you, plans to give you hope and a future."
Jeremiah 29:11

*L*et's listen to Hayley as she describes her recent date with Kevin:

Our greatest date didn't start out so great. Kevin had said, "Let's go over to the lake and watch the sunset." *But how can you watch a sunset when it's overcast and foggy?* I thought.

Kevin was so determined that I humored him. We got to the lake, and he pulled out a blanket and picnic basket. *Was this guy really serious?* There was no sun anywhere on the horizon; in fact, it was chilly. I felt weird trying to watch a sunset in the fog.

Kevin was acting strange—really nervous. "I'll be right back," he said and disappeared. So I sat on this blanket all alone. A few couples walked by hand-in-hand and stared at me. I felt really stupid. This date was going downhill fast. And then I heard a commotion behind me.

I turned around just in time to see a knight in a suit of armor riding a horse right toward me. As I looked more closely, I could see it was Kevin! He dismounted, and the next thing I knew he was on his knees asking me to marry me! Without a doubt, this was our greatest date yet!

What has been your greatest date? Have you had a unique story-book date like Hayley and Kevin? Or maybe you have had lots of great dates and now are looking forward to having a fairy-tale wedding where you will both ride off into the sunset to be blissfully happy ever after. Sounds like the end of the story, doesn't it? Not so. Your wedding day will only be the beginning of the story of your marriage.

A marriage is not a one-day event. Instead, marriage is a lifelong process of growing together and deepening your love for one another. It is facing life's trials together and pulling together in the good times as well as the bad. And, to be frank, marriage is not a fairy tale; it is more like the novel *War and Peace*. But the marriage relationship can be the most rewarding and fulfilling one you will ever know. And your greatest dates may be up ahead—after you're married!

CONSIDERING MATRIMONY?

Maybe like Hayley and Kevin, you've made the commitment to become engaged and are looking forward to getting married. Or maybe you are not engaged at this point but are wondering if you'd like to be. In either case, this date is going to help you look at your hopes and dreams for the future and better understand your expectations for marriage.

Many couples who marry are incredulous when marriage turns out to be different from what they expected. We don't want to shatter your hopes and dreams, but we do want you to take a good look at your present relationship and your expectations for the future. Too many who are considering marriage answer positively the premarital inventory question, "I expect my partner to change some of his/her behaviors after we marry."

Also it's important to note that every engaged couple does not end up marrying. One of the major purposes of marriage preparation is to help couples make a good decision about whether or not they are ready to be married to each other at this time. Couples who begin marriage preparation a year to eight months before marriage have a 15 to 17 percent rate of postponing or canceling the wedding if their preparation includes both an inventory and an educational program.[1]

The value of marriage preparation is having the opportunity to reexamine and reconfirm your decision to marry. In the following dates we want to help you look closer at your own decision to consider marriage or a more serious relationship and to better understand your own "good match." We will start that process on Date One by looking realistically at your own expectations.

What We Expected

We (the Arps) started marriage with stars in our eyes and a belief that we would surely always meet each other's needs. We got married in the middle of our college experience. The year was 1962. Our world was traumatized by the Cuban Missile Crisis. The Russian missiles were headed for Cuba, and the United States had its blockade in position. We were attending different colleges in different towns: Dave was in Atlanta at Georgia Tech; Claudia was in Athens at the University of Georgia. We were convinced if we didn't marry right away, the world would blow up and that we might never get to live together as husband and wife. So we did it. We got married without any premarital counseling, inventories, or any of the other helps available today. We were just going to live on our "love."

Then when the honeymoon was over and our hormones settled down, we discovered that marriage was not quite what we expected. Little things irritated us. I (Dave) was raised in a military home and assumed Claudia would be as orderly as I was. One of our first arguments was about how to arrange the magazines on the coffee table. I wanted them at right angles. Claudia wanted them to look more informal and "homey." I kept putting them at right angles; Claudia kept changing them to "her way." And hangers should be one inch apart in the closet—or so I thought. Claudia assumed just hanging up the clothes was a big accomplishment. So we immediately realized we would need to do some compromising.

When we (the Browns) were seriously dating and considering marriage, we just wanted to be together, and we never got around to discussing our expectations. We also married while still in college, and our unspoken expectations were based on the only marriages we knew well—those of our parents, which couldn't have been more different.

I (Curt) expected Natelle to be a wonderful cook who would never use a mix! My mother served home-cooked meals precisely at 7 A.M., noon, and 6 P.M. She dusted and vacuumed daily. I always had a drawer full of clean socks and underwear, and my shirts and jeans were always freshly laundered and ironed. Naturally, I assumed Natelle would be as passionate about housekeeping as my mother was. (Save the rotten eggs—I changed my view long ago!)

I (Natelle) had a totally different perspective. My mother was a high school English teacher and the first female high school principal in the state of Nebraska. She had worked outside the home since I was two years old. My dad enjoyed tinkering with the car, fixing leaky faucets, and hanging Christmas tree lights. He occasionally even helped with the cooking and was great with us kids. I assumed Curt would encourage me professionally and divide household chores equally. And, of course, he would be the handyman around the house just like my father was. After marriage it didn't take long for us to discover that we didn't exactly fit into the roles the other had hoped we would!

What are your expectations for your marriage? Listen to what some others contemplating marriage expected:

- *I expect my partner to always understand and encourage me.*
- *Our marriage will always make us happy.*
- *After marriage, our problems will go away.*
- *We will talk about everything, and therefore we will avoid serious disputes.*
- *With two incomes, we will be financially secure—especially since two can live almost as cheaply as one.*
- *We'll keep doing the same fun activities we presently do together.*
- *Our love life will always be exciting and satisfying.*
- *We will divide and conquer housework fifty-fifty.*
- *I expect my mate to meet my needs—to be a lot like me.*

Obviously, these people were shocked when their mates were unable to live up to their expectations. It is really important that we talk about our expectations. It is hard enough to meet expectations when we know what they are, but it's impossible when we don't.

What You Expect

Do you identify with any of the comments above? On Date One you will have the opportunity to take our Expectation Survey and talk about what is really important to you. When Lisa and Ben talked through their Expectation Survey, they discovered areas where their expectations were totally different. For example, Ben had little need for "intellectual closeness"—that was the last on his list. But for Lisa, it was near the top of her list and she would probably starve to death without it! On the other hand, Lisa rated "mutual activity" lower than Ben. Talking about their expectations before marriage was a very helpful exercise. They understood that they would have to work to adjust their expectations and that their marriage would benefit from their different interests. Lisa would learn to put a higher value on shared activities while Ben would appreciate how important it was to Lisa for him to relate to her on an intellectual level.

You too can benefit from understanding your differing hopes, dreams, and expectations—especially when you talk about them before marriage. But first we suggest that you consider what your own expectations are for your *10 Great Dates.*

If you are engaged, we hope you expect to have some fun, to learn more about each other, and also to pick up new relationship skills that will help your future marriage succeed. And if you are seriously dating, we hope your expectations for these dates include helping you understand each other better and equipping you to be able to make an informed and wise decision about your future together. Whether or not you are engaged, these dates can help you see your relationship more clearly, evaluate your present skills and abilities you bring to this potential partnership, and learn new relational skills.

So let's get started! But before we look to the future, let's consider the past and how you got to where you are today in your relationship.

LOOKING BACK — CELEBRATING GREAT MEMORIES TOGETHER

Let's take a trip down memory lane and revisit the day you met. Do you remember the first time you saw each other? We (the Arps) won't ever forget the day we first met.

I was thirteen, and Dave, who was fifteen, threw me into the swimming pool with my clothes on! But we were first attracted to each other when we met again after I graduated from high school. After finishing his freshman year at Georgia Tech, Dave was again spending the summer with his grandmother who lived in Ellijay, Georgia—the same small north Georgia town where I grew up. A mutual friend got us together, and it was almost love at first sight. Dave's impish nature was still in full force, but he was also fun-loving, adventurous, and a college man!

And Dave thought Claudia's vivaciousness, enthusiasm for life, and twinkle in her eyes were irresistible. Within three weeks we were together and never looked back (or at anyone else!).

It's fun to think back on our own history and remember the excitement of that time when we realized we were in love. Memories help us to remember just how important our marriage is and why we want to keep nurturing our relationship.

CELEBRATING THE PRESENT

From our observations, when couples become engaged, most of their time and energy are focused on planning the wedding. Often they forget to nurture their relationship now. In our Before You Say "I Do" seminar, we give couples the opportunity to celebrate the present by considering three questions.

The first question you might ponder is "What is great about your relationship right now?" These are the positive attributes of your relationship to be celebrated. Perhaps you work hard at expressing your true feelings to each other, or maybe you look for ways to encourage the other. These are the attributes to celebrate! Cheri and Bill are seriously considering marriage. When they did this exercise their list included the following positives:

- We have similar interests.
- Our faith in God is important to both of us.
- We laugh together a lot.
- We're good at expressing concerns and work together to deal with them.

The second question we suggest is "What is okay about our relationship, but could be better?" One thing Cheri wrote down is that she gets irritated when Bill says he will meet her at specific times but is continually ten minutes late. Bill honestly can't see why being ten minutes late is such a big deal.

The third question, "What is one thing you can do to make your relationship better?" helped Cheri and Bill move forward with this issue. Bill already knows one thing he can do to make their relationship better. If he will more realistically estimate his time of arrival and call when he's running late, perhaps Cheri will be more understanding when he is late and give him some slack.

LOOKING FORWARD — CELEBRATING THE FUTURE

Many couples anticipating marriage have a "future focus." It is exciting to look forward to marriage and dream of how wonderful it will be, but it is also wise to be realistic and articulate some of your expectations. Now is the time to take some steps to insure that your future is based on solid principles.

In our national survey of long-term marriages, we found three common strands in marriages that are alive and healthy. First, they put their relationship with each other first; second, both spouses are committed to growing and changing together; and third, they work at staying close.

Put Your Relationship First

At this point in your relationship, putting your relationship first is obvious, but after you say "I do," life happens—careers, children, sports, hobbies, friends, church activities, or whatever will vie for your time and attention. Throughout a marriage, partners must continue to refocus their lives on each other and make their relationship with each other a higher priority than other relationships or activities.

Most would probably agree that the marriage relationship should be a top priority, but sometimes in days, hours, and minutes, it just doesn't work out that way—even when we try. Love is a delicate balancing act. Some things we can control; others things we must juggle. You might want to think about your life right now. If you peel off the layers of activities and time commitments, what is underneath? Do you often have wistful thoughts about each other? Do you wisely use the time you do have?

Commit to Grow Together

Building a successful marriage includes a lifelong commitment to grow and change together. Unless you are really committed to your marriage, it is easy to give up when problems come along. Anyone who has been married for more than a few days knows that problems will surface. All marriages have problems, but the difference between those marriages that make it and those that don't is that the successful ones are committed to growing together and working to solve each problem that arises.

A commitment to growth goes beyond just sticking together. It is also a commitment to adapt to each other's changing needs. Ellen confided, "Jon and I have been married for only three years, yet we both have changed so much. If we change as much in the next three years, how can we stay close?"

Ellen's question is shared by many. We have observed that couples who refuse to grow and change will only have a mediocre marriage. Adapting to each other requires self-sacrifice. It calls for thinking of the other person and looking for ways to grow with and adapt to each other's changing needs. It means being each other's best friend—being that one person the other can always count on.

Work at Staying Close

Key to building a successful marriage is entering marriage with the expectation that it takes work to stay close. Unfortunately, many things tend to push us apart—like overcommitment or lack of sleep. We try to avoid negative situations as much as possible. For instance, when we find ourselves overcommitted once again, we try to pace ourselves and say no when we need to. When you have a choice to make, a good question to ask yourself is "Will this action or attitude bring us closer together, or will it put distance in our relationship?" A key to enriching marriage is simply learning to say no!

Working at staying close will help you build your love relationship. You can stay close by focusing on helping your partner. Any help you offer each other will help your marriage partnership. Any pain, hurt, insult, any lack of support or faithfulness, and any failure to help your partner will reflect back on your marriage. You can be the most positive reinforcing person in each other's lives if you are willing to enter marriage with the expectation and desire to put your relationship first, to grow together, and to work at staying close.

Now it's time for your first date. Turn to Date One in the Dating Guide and expect to have a great date talking about your hopes, dreams, and expectations.

Date Two

Appreciating Your Differences

I got gaps; you got gaps; we fill each other's gaps.
Rocky

Our (the Browns') differences surfaced soon after we married. When we were engaged, we would do anything just to be together. I (Curt) would even go shopping with Natelle. But after getting married, I realized I really didn't like to shop.

One Saturday morning sticks in my mind. It was early winter, and Natelle decided she needed a new winter coat. She asked me to go along with her to the mall. I'm thinking, *This won't take too long. Just go to a couple of stores, buy a coat, and come home.* Boy, was I wrong! We arrived at the mall and started walking toward a coat store. We walked by a shoe store, and Natelle noticed some shoes she liked, so we went inside to look. Finally, we left the shoe store, and once again started toward the coat store. We walked by a bookstore, and Natelle remembered a book she was looking for—another twenty-minute detour!

By this time I'm going crazy. *What do shoes and books have to do with buying a winter coat?* I just can't relate. I have the "hunting" instinct that says, "If you are hunting for a coat, go straight to the coat store, buy a coat, and take your coat home." Simple, right? Not for Natelle. She thinks browsing is part of the whole shopping experience. We have been married almost thirty years, so we've learned to navigate our differences, but we still view shopping through different filters—and probably always will.

GENDER DIFFERENCES

Are our different shopping styles based on gender or personality differences? Do you know men who like to shop? We do. A great deal of research now exists on the differences between male and female, both biologically and psychologically.

We are different. After all, God created us male and female. Eve was not just another Adam. In Genesis 1:27 we read, "So God created man in his own image, in the image of God he created him; male and female he created them." Amazing as it is, we are created different, yet together we can reflect God's image. Together the genders can complement one another. And that's our goal in marriage—to complement and not compete with one another, to really appreciate our differences.

A summary of some of the latest research on gender differences can be found in the book *Fighting for Your Marriage*. But the authors caution us: "When we talk about gender differences we want to say something very important about research on differences between men and women. We are talking about broad average differences between groups. So in talking about differences between men and women we would add the words 'on average' to just about any statement. The differences between men and women in marriage have been highly inflated ... men and women are a lot more similar in what they want out of marriage than they are different." Their overall advice is, "If you want to have a great relationship, the way you handle your differences matters more than what those differences are."[1]

Gender differences exist, but so do personality differences, and when you look at the ways you are alike and the ways you are different, you hit both personality and gender-related differences.

If you want to pursue gender differences further, refer to the list of books in Helpful Resources on page 141. For Date Two we will concentrate on looking at the ways we are alike and the ways we are different.

PERSONALITY DIFFERENCES

Have you heard the old adage "Opposites attract"? This was definitely true in our experience.

I (Claudia) remember when we met. Dave was so laid-back and easy-going. He had all the time in the world to listen to me talk, and he never looked at his watch! Just being with him caused me to relax. He didn't take life as seriously as I did, and he could always make me laugh and loosen up.

I (Dave) was attracted to Claudia's energy and enthusiasm for life. She was perky and had numerous ideas of things to do, places to go, and people to see. It was exciting being around her. I do have a great listening ear, and it was fun to listen to Claudia talk for hours on end. I liked to listen; she liked to talk. Great combination!

Then we were married. Guess what? The differences that originally attracted us to each other over time became irritations. Now in Claudia's eyes, Dave was slow and at times unmotivated. And so not time-oriented! He would forget the time and be late meeting her for an appointment. Being the more serious-minded, introspective one, Claudia was sure he had been killed in a car accident.

And how was Dave adjusting to the five-ring circus he married? He soon tired of Claudia's endless plans—frankly, some of her suggestions felt more like manipulation to him—so he often resisted going along with her. At times Claudia's endless chatter irritated him. Did she have to talk all the time? What was wrong with just having a quiet evening at home?

I LOVE YOU. YOU'RE PERFECT. NOW CHANGE.

When what initially attracted us to each other became irritations, we tried to change each other. It just didn't work. I didn't understand why Claudia couldn't just laugh things off and not take life so seriously. Claudia wanted me to be more introspective and analytical.

And then we made a job change that required us to take a battery of psychological tests. We still remember the day we completed those tests. I nonchalantly checked off my answers while watching a football game on television. Claudia carefully thought through each answer and cross-checked them for consistency.

The next week we were interviewed by Dr. Blaudau, a psychologist. He sat at his desk, looking at our test results. "Dave, here are your strong points." As he listed them, I began to feel better and better. He went on, "Now here are the areas in which you are weak." That wasn't nearly as enjoyable for me to hear, but Dr. Blaudau was right on target!

Then he went through the same procedure with Claudia, listing her strengths and weaknesses. Looking at both of us, he said, "Dave and Claudia, here are the areas you agree on, and here are the areas in which you tend to have problems." He could have been a fly on our walls—he didn't miss anything. My respect for psychological tests went up about 300 percent. Then he gave us one of the most beneficial challenges of our lives: "You probably have noticed, Dave, that your weak areas are Claudia's strengths, and, Claudia, your weak areas are Dave's strengths. If you will allow each other to operate in your areas of strengths and not be threatened by the other, you have the potential for building a great marriage partnership."

We would like to say that we went right out and applied his advice instantly—but it didn't happen quite like that. It was hard for both of us to admit that our weaknesses were our partner's strengths. It took time and practice, and at times it was awkward, but we took Dr. Blaudau's challenge seriously. We knew that if we could follow his advice, we would be a stronger team.

PRACTICING BALANCE

We haven't always agreed about how our finances should be handled. In the past this has led to tension and frustration. But after Dr. Blaudau challenged us to balance our strengths, we decided we would try to change how we handled our money.

First, we evaluated our strengths. Dave has a mathematical engineering background—he's detail-oriented—so we decided that he would handle the basic accounting. It is his job to update our finances on the computer. Balancing bank accounts, paying bills, and dealing with income tax returns are just easier for him than for Claudia. This doesn't mean Claudia has nothing to say about our finances. Together we set our budget and make major financial decisions.

Claudia is the chief shopper. She can spot a bargain four stores away. She stretches our household dollars and does most of the grocery shopping. When Dave grocery shops, he's likely to come home with fifteen cans of soup and his favorite high-fat, tasty snacks but without the needed milk and bread.

Do we always agree about our finances and grocery shopping lists? Of course not, but we have learned to communicate, compromise, and develop our own plan for how we earn, save, give, and spend our money. Working together has been a plus, especially in our finances.

You may want to assess your strengths and weaknesses and consider how you can encourage each other to operate in areas of strength as much as possible. It is not necessary to take a battery of psychological tests, but we do encourage you to take advantage of one of the several excellent premarital inventories that will help you discover your own couple assets. Two that we highly recommend are PREPARE and FOCCUS (see Appendix page 139).

IDENTIFY YOUR COUPLE STRENGTHS

On Date Two you will have the opportunity to begin identifying your strengths as a couple. We believe our different strengths can help us balance each other—especially if we appreciate those differences and don't feel threatened by them. In areas where you have similar strengths, you may want to look for ways to work together harmoniously. To build a strong marriage, partners need to learn how to appreciate and use the ways they are alike and the ways they are different.

On this date you will have the opportunity to consider seven continuums that illustrate some human polarities. We suggest that you think about your own relationship as you look at each continuum. Both sides of each have strengths and weaknesses, advantages and disadvantages. We believe that which side you or your partner is on is less important than understanding that people are different. Seeing where you are on each can help you identify your assets, balance each other, and see that differences are okay. Also, from time to time, you may find you are at different places on these continuums. For example, in some groups you may be very extroverted, and at other times, quiet and introverted.

Here's our suggestion: Think of each continuum as a seesaw, place yourself and your partner on the graphics that accompany each section, and consider how you might balance each other. If you are both on the same side of the continuum, you will want to think about how you can compensate for a weakness you both have.

Feelings-Oriented/Facts-Oriented

Feelings-oriented people express feelings and emotions easily. They like an open atmosphere, and if tension enters the relationship, they strive to clear the air. They desire to work through conflict and "not let the sun go down on their anger." They need feedback from the other.

Feelings-oriented people are more interested in the relationship than the facts.

Facts-oriented people speak to express ideas and to communicate information more than to express feelings. They would rather not express or acknowledge unpleasant feelings and even become uncomfortable when emotional subjects arise, preferring peaceful coexistence to being confronted with emotions. They are more goal-oriented than people-oriented.

Your different perspectives can be beneficial. Suppose you are trying to reach a solution to a certain problem and one of you is more facts-oriented and the other is more feelings-oriented. On the one hand, a decision made purely on feelings may be problematic. On the other hand, a decision based entirely on cognitive information may ignore important input. One way of thinking is not more or less important than the other.

You can achieve balance in your own relationship by identifying where you both are coming from. We suggest that you place yourself on this continuum. Are you generally more feelings-oriented or more facts-oriented? Where is your partner on this continuum?

FEELINGS-ORIENTED   FACTS-ORIENTED

I (Dave) am actually more feelings-oriented than Claudia, who tends to be more facts-oriented. I'm sensitive to what's going on emotionally. It was easier for me to identify with our children—especially during their teens—while Claudia, with her cognitive approach, kept our ship moving forward. As parents and partners, we discovered we make better decisions together when we talk about both the emotions and facts.

If you are both feelings-oriented or both facts-oriented, you might want to consider how you can compensate. If you are both feelings-oriented, it's easy to get caught up in the excitement of the moment and overlook facts, like newlyweds Whitney and Derek. They both got carried away while shopping for a new car and committed themselves to buying a brand new Toyota Camry on a used-car budget. They ignored their financial reality and ended up with large car payments that drained their limited budget. The next time they shop for a car, they will compensate for their weakness by doing their financial homework and deciding just how much they can spend before they hit the car lots.

On the other hand, if you are both facts-oriented, it may be easy for you to make a decision based solely on facts. If Whitney and Derek based their car decision only on the facts, they may have purchased a car they could afford but that they both hated to drive.

So next time you face an important decision, you may want to talk about both the factual and emotional aspects of the issue. If you are facts-oriented, you may have to dig a little deeper to unearth the emotional issues.

Private/Public

We have observed that public people are energized by being around people while private people are energized by being alone. How are you energized? What energizes you as a couple?

Privates naturally like to be alone and to have time alone as a couple. They shy away from groups. Nathan and Hannah have been married for six months and are both privates. They would love to live on a desert island and have little to do with others. Nathan and Hannah naturally protect their private times, but they could benefit from more time with others. We suggested that they join a couples' small group study or a softball team, or make a list of couples they would like to get to know, and from time to time invite one couple over for dinner or dessert.

Ellen and Marshall, married for two years with no children, are just the opposite. Both are publics. For them the more people the better. What's a vacation without friends along? They are energized by others, care deeply for others, and are involved in other people's lives. To achieve balance, Ellen and Marshall need to plan time alone. Relationships are built in twos, and they need to be sure to plan enough "two" time to keep theirs healthy and growing.

Olivia and Scott have been married for two years and are at opposite ends of the continuum. Scott loves people and is continually inviting others to be a part of meals, vacations, and other outings. Olivia is more private and just wants to be with Scott. One of her favorite tricks is to kidnap Scott for an overnight getaway. Scott and Olivia work to find balance by respecting each other's preferences and trying to have both types of interactions. Where are you on this continuum?

PRIVATE   *PUBLIC*

At times when we become over-involved with others, we have to regroup and plan time. Sometimes we look at the previous month's calendar to check how we're doing. This helps us plan for the next month.

Nathan and Hannah, the private couple from our seminar, now compensate by planning a couple of activities each month that include others. Last month they invited another couple to go to the flea market with them.

If you are opposites, you may want to think about how you can balance each other. For instance, each could plan one activity for the next few weeks. One might choose having friends over for dinner and the other might plan a date to go hiking on a secluded path.

Spontaneous/Planner

Spontaneous people are first cousins to the feelings-oriented people. Life tends to just happen, unfettered by daily drudgery. Spontaneity is a way of life. As a result, the fun, exciting things get done. The more mundane side of life—like menu planning, paying the bills, or housecleaning—may be ignored.

Planners like structure and may be threatened by too much ambiguity. They are usually orderly and prefer to do things the same way time and time again. Interruptions are irritating if they prevent carrying out the daily plan. Planners need a gentle push to expand their horizons.

Where are you on this continuum?

SPONTANEOUS   *PLANNER*

If you are both spontaneous, you might agree to check with each other before making any new commitments. If you're both planners, you could surprise your partner. Whatever you plan will be "planned" for you but will be spontaneous for your partner!

If you're opposites, can you think of ways you might balance each other? Maybe the planner can defer to the spontaneous one, who says, "Why cook dinner tonight? Let's go out to eat." On the other hand, the spontaneous one can agree to sit down and write out meal plans for the next week, such as, "Let's grill fish next Friday."

Live-Wire/Laid-Back

Live-wires are continually in motion. If those around them are not focused, they will happily help organize them. They have an abundance of ideas and the energy to put many into motion.

Laid-back people are easy to be around. They are flexible and rarely get rattled with life. They are not as directive as live-wires, but they exert influence in other ways. They usually have a great listening ear, which is one reason many successful counselors have these attributes.

We are opposites. Claudia is the live-wire. Her definition of "boring" is having nothing to do. She doesn't like to take naps during the day—she might miss something. Dave would much rather just let life happen. He marches to a slower (but more consistent) drummer. He is methodical, persistent, and likes to cross all the t's and dot all the i's.

On this continuum we benefit from each other's perspective and balance each other most of the time. But not all of the time! When Claudia gets super-focused on a project, she loses all track of time and can work nonstop for hours without a break. Dave will stop in the middle and take a fifteen-minute nap, which drives Claudia crazy. When we are working together to meet a deadline, Claudia will just hit the high points, and Dave will get upset because the details are missing!

Where do you fall on the following continuum?

LIVE-WIRE   *LAID-BACK*

If you are both live-wires or both laid-back, can you think of ways you might compensate? Do you need to slow down or speed up? Do you need to cut back on your eighteen-hour days? If you are opposites, how can you balance each other? One way we balance each other is that Dave oversees details that demand consistency, like keeping up with our monthly obligations and managing our calendar, while Claudia moves us toward the big picture. She, on the one hand, is the one to say, "Let's talk about our commitments for next year and how much traveling is reasonable." Dave, on the other hand, would say, "What about the details of today?" Dave calms Claudia down when she gets hyper, and she motivates him to be a little more pro-active.

Night Owl/Day Lark

Why do so many night owls hang out with and marry day larks? In our own observations, it really helps couples survive their children's baby and teenage years. The night owl gets the night duty. Psychologists tell us we are born with an innate time orientation. What is yours? When is your most productive time of the day? Morning? Afternoon? Evening?

This continuum may be the easiest to identify but the hardest to balance. We (the Arps) first tried to change each other—it didn't work. But over the years we continue to work on harmonizing our clocks. Claudia's eyes automatically close about the time mine pop open. My creative time is between 11 P.M. and 2 A.M., while Claudia's best time is early in the morning.

For us, one benefit to being opposites in this area is that it gives us space in our relationship. We work closely together for long hours. Sometimes Claudia likes to slip off to bed early, and at times I like to delve into one of my midnight projects.

When we (the Browns) tried to decide which one of us is the night owl and which one of us is the day lark, we determined that Natelle is both and I am neither! We definitely require different amounts of sleep.

Consequently, Natelle often stays up later at night and gets up earlier in the morning than I do. She actually did the math and calculated that I have slept over a year more than she has. Natelle kids me by saying, "Just think of the things I have accomplished with my extra time—books read, menus planned, Bible study lessons completed, and letters and emails written!"

On the other hand, I tell her that I have gotten more done in less time because I am well rested and focused. And who knows, I might even live a year longer than I would have without that extra sleep!

What about you? Where do you fall on this continuum?

NIGHT OWL   *DAY LARK*

If you are both night owls or both day larks, you might want to think about ways you can compensate. At times your job or circumstance may play an important role in how you adapt to your own time-orientation. One of our night-owl friends is a surgeon who must get up early for surgery or hospital calls. His wife, also a night owl, tries to adjust her schedule. On vacations and off-the-job times, they can stay up all night and sleep all day!

Time-Oriented/Not Time-Oriented

Here is another continuum where we are different. As we indicated earlier, I (Dave) am the classic "non-timed" person. Like the popular author Garrison Keillor, I am just "happy to be here." Time—what's that? Claudia's solution helped. Once she gave me a watch with three alarms, and at times I have used all three of them. (But I still had to remember why I set them!)

We learn from each other. Claudia has relaxed. Sometimes she can be ten minutes late without stressing out. We both get to weddings on time, and I have graduated to a one-alarm watch. Where are you on this continuum?

TIME-ORIENTED   *NOT TIME-ORIENTED*

If you are both time-oriented or both not time-oriented, you may want to think about how you can compensate in the future. Alarm clocks, alarm watches, notes to yourself, and an efficient secretary may help. If you are opposites, you may want to consider how you can balance each other.

Saver/Spender

Another continuum deals with one's approach to money. Some are energized by saving money. Others are energized by spending it.

Katie and Josh are considering marriage and are already struggling with being on opposite ends of the spender/saver continuum. Katie came from a family where money grew on trees. If there were blank checks in the checkbook, there must be money in the checking account. Josh's penny-pinching family gave "frugal" a new meaning. They dried paper towels to reuse! Katie and Josh plan to combine their finances after marriage, so they will have to work hard to balance Katie's tendency to be a spendthrift and Josh's tendency to be a hoarder.

SAVER   *SPENDER*

Where would you place yourself on this continuum? More important than where each of you may be on the chart is whether you are
willing to work together to find balance. Actually, if you are on opposite
ends of this seesaw, it may be easier for you to find balance than if you
are both savers or both spenders. If you are both spenders, it will be
very important for you to agree to live by a budget (see Date Five).

WHAT ABOUT THE WEAKNESSES?

Our goal is not to be the same; we were created with differences.
But one skill that is important to develop if you want to build a
successful marriage is to accept each other and benefit from your
differing strengths and accept each other's weaknesses. If you find that
one of you dominates most of the continuums, or concentrates on the
other's weaknesses, you may want to set aside some time to do some
reevaluating.

Concentrating on weaknesses is like poking an open sore. It doesn't
bring healing. Over the past twenty-five years of leading our marriage
seminars, we have observed that couples are helped much more by
concentrating on their combined strengths, seeing these as their couple
assets, than by pointing out their weaknesses. When partners concentrate on each other's strengths, an amazing thing happens. They learn
from each other.

Let us share one more observation. A strength taken to an
extreme can also be a weakness, so we would encourage you to strive
for balance. A perfectionist so intensely into details may never get
anything accomplished. As a couple you have the wonderful opportunity to balance each other and combine your assets, but you need
to be prepared to handle some inappropriate reactions both from
yourself and from your partner (see Date Four).

Psychologist Revisited

Years later, we (the Arps) had the opportunity to retake those
psychological tests and to sit down again with Dr. Blaudau. We were
surprised and pleased to learn that we actually had learned from each
other. Our weak areas were not as weak. We were a stronger team. We
had proven it works! We challenge you to prove it for yourself. Work
for unity in your diversity, and you too can be a strong team.

Do you see ways your differences complement each other and may give balance to your future marriage partnership? Together you can discover ways to compensate for areas in which you may be too much alike. Appreciate the uniqueness of your team. You can build a wonderful partnership based on your differences.

Look for the hidden assets of your team. Be willing to continue to learn and grow together. You will be amazed at the couple treasures you will discover! Amazingly, we discovered our greatest assets are our differences. Now get ready to talk about them.

> *Turn to Date Two in the Dating Guide.*
> *A great date on appreciating*
> *your differences awaits you!*

Date Three

Communicating and Connecting

Let your conversation be always full of grace, seasoned with salt,
so that you may know how to answer everyone.
Colossians 4:6

Before marriage Alexia and Shawn dreamed about purchasing their first house and how romantic it would be to fix it up together.

And sure enough, a few months after the wedding they found a small, yet charming, fixer-upper at a reasonable price. When they began talking about the vast possibilities for remodeling and redecorating, they quickly discovered they had different ideas and priorities. Shawn wanted to immediately strip the wallpaper and paint the bedroom. Alexia wanted to start with the kitchen, replacing the old kitchen linoleum with vinyl. Shawn wanted to wait until they could afford wood flooring.

A couple of months into their refurbishing efforts, Shawn suggested to Alexia that they host an open house for their friends. She agreed that when all the fixing up was complete they would have a great party. The next day a friend of Shawn's called, and Alexia overheard Shawn say, "Sure, we'll be ready for the open house next weekend. Hope you can come."

When Shawn hung up, Alexia said, "How could you possibly set a date without talking to me first? What were you thinking? How could you think we could do an open house so soon? We're nowhere close to being finished, and I'm definitely not ready to start entertaining!"

"Well, I am!" Shawn responded. "You'll never be ready—things will never be perfect enough for you!"

Deadlocked, disconnected, and frustrated, Alexia and Shawn showed up at the Browns' door for some "post 'I do'" help. As they talked about their situation, they calmed down a bit. They obviously needed some help in communicating and connecting.

THREE PATTERNS OF COMMUNICATION

We have found that our relationship is only as intimate as the conversations we have with each other. Words can help to build a deeper relationship, or they can destroy the very foundations of your marriage. Understanding three patterns of communication—chatting, confronting, and connecting—may help you identify your present communication patterns and choose more helpful patterns for the future.

Pattern One: Chatting

Chatting refers to surface conversations. "Where do you want to go for dinner tonight?" "Do you think it is going to rain today?" "What color do you think would be best to paint the bedroom?" "Have you seen the screwdriver?" Chatting is part of healthy conversations. We chat every day. Chatting is safe—no sparks fly—but when chatting is as deep as communication goes, it is a shallow and lonely pattern.

Pattern Two: Confronting

The confronting pattern is the attacking style of communication. "You" statements and "why" questions attack and make other people want to defend themselves. Here are a few examples: "You make me so angry!" "You're so inconsiderate." "You never think of me!" "Why did you invite your friends to come over without asking me first?" "Who made you the boss?" In the confronting pattern, it is easy to be negative and get into a shouting match.

When Alexia attacked Shawn, his natural response was to defend himself, "If we wait until you are ready to have an open house, it'll never happen. Why can't you be a bit more flexible?"

From time to time we slip into the confronting mode. The problem arises when this type of communication becomes a pattern. Our goal whenever we get into the confronting mode is to get out of it as quickly as we can!

Make a Contract

To log less time in the confronting pattern of communication, we suggest making a contract to never attack each other intentionally. This contract has two simple parts[1]:

1. We will not intentionally attack each other.
2. We will not defend ourselves.

In other words, we agree that we will not intentionally use the confronting communication pattern. And on those occasions when we slip and attack the other, the one who feels attacked can diffuse the confrontation by choosing to take the higher road and resisting the desire to justify or defend our position. We can say, "Hey, we have a contract not to attack each other."

Please note that "We will not defend ourselves" does not mean allowing, enabling, or enduring abusive behavior. Instead we are suggesting that you can choose to stop the escalation of anger by refusing to respond back in the confronting pattern—to say, "That sounded like an attacking statement to me."

This contract helps us to move on to a more helpful pattern of communication and one that can enrich and deepen our relationship. If Alexia and Shawn had had this contract before their blowup, they could have gotten back on track sooner. After signing their contract, Alexia and Shawn came up with a "code" word to remind each other about their contract.

One code word we use is simply to say, "Ouch, I feel a pinch!" This alerts the other person that whether it was intended or not, you felt attacked. A wise partner will accept this reminder, back off, and honor the contract.

In a recent seminar, when we discussed the confronting pattern, the group brainstormed different signals they could use to alert their partner. One couple shared how they use the phrase, "Butter, butter." The group laughed and we thought that it was a silly signal.

Fast forward a few days. We were in the car when once again Dave forgot to buckle his seatbelt—(this is one of our little perpetual issues)—so I simply said, "Butter, butter." Dave looked puzzled and then laughed and buckled his seatbelt.

Let us encourage you to use whatever signal that works for you—even a nonsense signal can dispel tension and remind you it's time to leave the confronting pattern and move on to a more helpful one. After Alexia and Shawn agreed to make the contract with each other not to attack each other or defend themselves, they were ready to move on to the "working" pattern of communication—the connecting pattern.

Pattern Three: Connecting

With the connecting pattern of communication you can deepen your relationship, become intimate, close companions, and even resolve differences.

Connecting communication begins with a willingness to share our true self with our partner—to make ourselves vulnerable by letting the other know our most intimate thoughts and feelings. Our contract to not attack each other or defend ourselves allows us to share our true feelings without becoming negative. We know the other will handle our feelings tenderly and will not defend, justify, or attack when we make ourselves vulnerable. This opens the door for true intimate conversations. Sharing our feelings on a deeper level helps build a strong communication system that enables us to handle the problems when they come along.

The Feelings Formula[2]

We would like to suggest a simple formula for expressing feelings that we have taught to thousands of couples. It is clear, simple, and non-threatening when used with the right attitude.

"Let me tell you how I feel."

The first part of the formula is to state clearly, directly, and in love, "Let me tell you how I feel. I feel. . ." (fill in with a word that describes how you feel—frustrated, angry, alone, hurt, disappointed, anxious, happy, joyful). Express your inward feelings and emotions, and avoid attacking the other person.

Using the feelings formula Alexia might say, "I feel frustrated when we aren't anywhere near ready for an open house and you go ahead and invite people." "I feel devalued when we don't make important decisions together." Or, "I feel manipulated and coerced into having an open house."

In using the feelings formula, don't confuse "I feel" with "I think." If you can substitute "I think" for "I feel," then it is not a feeling. For instance, "I feel that you hurt me!" expresses a thought and judgment. It is the confronting pattern in disguise. Much better would be to direct the statement toward yourself and say, "I feel hurt when this happens." You can also state your feelings by using the words, "I am," as in "I am hurt when this happens."

Remember, the goal is to express inward feelings and emotions that reflect back on the speaker and that avoid attacking the other person. Feelings are neither right nor wrong; they simply are there; however, it is valuable to know how the other feels. This leads to the second part of the feelings formula.

"Now tell me how you feel."

After stating clearly and in love how you feel, the next step is to ask your partner, "Now tell me how you feel." Then really listen. As you are listening, it is important not to judge your partner's feelings.

At this point, Shawn might say something like, "I feel misunderstood. I'm proud of the work we have done so far on our house and just want to show it off."

Feelings are fragile, and it is important to handle them with care. But if we can get to the real issue through sharing our feelings, we can attack the problem instead of each other and, at the same time, strengthen our own marriage. Alexia was beginning to understand this wasn't a power struggle and that Shawn, who is more spontaneous than she is, just wanted to show off their progress. Shawn was beginning to understand that, to Alexia, having people come to an open house before they were finished was a huge pressure on her. She was embarrassed that everything would not be completed.

But We Are So Different!

Even when using the more helpful connecting pattern of communication, the way you use it may be very different. You can let your differences enhance your conversations and help you connect. For instance, suppose one of you really likes to get things out in the open while the other reflects before speaking and takes time to get beyond too much anger and hurt. On the other hand, the one who holds things in can become moody and the one who speaks up more quickly can help to bring things out into the open before anger escalates. Our differing

ways of communicating and connecting are influenced by our personalities and also by our childhood experiences.

Family of Origin Factor

We are greatly influenced by the communication patterns of our
family of origin. If you grew up in a family with excellent communication skills and eagerness to share feelings and the deeper issues of life
with one another, you are probably a great communicator. But what if
you grew up in a family who never really communicated with each other
or every discussion was an argument? Not to panic, it is possible to
unlearn the negative confronting style and learn the more positive
connecting style.

Mackenzie and Andrew have been married for a year and have
difficulty communicating and connecting in a meaningful way. Andrew,
an only child, grew up in a military family. His dad's attitude toward
sharing feelings was, "If you were supposed to have feelings, the Army
would have issued them to you!" His dad often used the confronting
pattern while his mom preferred chatter. She was very reserved, rarely
engaged him in meaningful dialogue, and usually communicated non-
verbally. From an early age Andrew knew "the look" that clued him in
that his mother was unhappy with him. Family discussions were logical
and unemotional, and Andrew was rarely asked for his opinion.

Mackenzie's family was just the opposite. Her parents, co-owners
of the leading local art gallery, were fun-loving and very expressive, and
they always encouraged Mackenzie to say whatever was on her mind.
Mackenzie's brother, who was pursuing an acting career, was also
expressive. Evening meals at Mackenzie's house were lively and entertaining. Feelings were to be shared and experienced by all.

It is not surprising that in the first few months after saying "I do,"
Andrew and Mackenzie struggled with their communication with each
other. Like her family of origin, Mackenzie was expressive and very
verbal. Andrew, reflecting his family of origin, preferred to avoid emotional talk and would withdraw when Mackenzie tried to engage him in
meaningful conversation.

We met Mackenzie and Andrew during their first year of marriage
when they attended our Marriage Alive seminar. When they were able
to identify the different patterns of communication, Andrew was able to
express his deeper thoughts and feelings through using the feelings

formula. Mackenzie better understood why Andrew was hesitant to say what he was really feeling. With this tool, they were able to make some good progress in improving their communication. Was it easy? No way!

At first Andrew complained, "This all sounds great, but I couldn't say how I felt if I wanted to—I just don't have the words! My dad hasn't said five words his whole life and none had anything to do with how he felt, and me? Well, I'm a chip off the old block."

To help Andrew venture into the world of feelings, we brainstormed words we could use to express our feelings. If you, like Andrew, have difficulty expressing feelings, maybe our list will help you get started.

I Feel . . .

hurt	*angry*	*frustrated*
happy	*threatened*	*lonely*
confused	*inspired*	*stressed*
loved	*depressed*	*confident*
excited	*anxious*	*proud*
belittled	*joyful*	*used*
peaceful	*attacked*	*energetic*
irritated	*sad*	*helpless*
content	*enlightened*	*responsible*
overwhelmed	*encouraged*	*remorseful*
left out	*broken*	*sick*
envious	*trapped*	*stifled*
squelched	*tense*	*betrayed*
nervous	*relaxed*	*silly*
grateful	*abused*	*calm*
creative	*scared*	*secure*
perplexed	*misunderstood*	*alone*
pressured	*burdened*	*afraid*
optimistic	*pessimistic*	*enthusiastic*
crushed	*numb*	*bored*
mad	*ignored*	*pleased*
uneasy	*deprived*	*embarrassed*

How comfortable are you with words like those above? Are you willing to try the feelings formula? Are there areas you hesitate to discuss? You may find it helpful to write down how you feel about an issue. You might want to try using the feelings formula and making sure you are stating your true feelings without attacking or blaming your partner. Tell your partner how you feel (or let your partner read what you wrote) and ask for his or her feelings in response. As your partner speaks, seek to understand the feeling about the issue.

For example, maybe you are concerned that even before marriage you both tend to abuse credit cards. You fear financial troubles are in your future and want to talk about it and find a solution now. Remember, the overused credit cards and your fear of financial trouble are the issues you want to attack. You might say or write something like, "I'm anxious and afraid that after we are married we will charge more on our credit cards than we can comfortably pay off. Do you feel the same way?"

Too Hard?

One seminar participant claimed, "This just isn't me! Besides, this seems fake and unnatural." Maybe you feel this way too. We understand. It wasn't easy for us either. Clear communication is hard work! It is hard to let the other know how you really feel. Just how will the other use that information?

At first when we tried to express our true feelings, it was easier for Claudia than for Dave. When Claudia said how she felt, Dave would counter with, "Why do you feel that way?" or, "No one in their right mind should feel that way!" Dave had to remember that feelings are neither right nor wrong, but knowing how the other feels is vital to developing a communication system that works. We found that expressing our feelings by using the feelings formula helped us attack the problem and not each other.

The next time you have strong negative feelings, you might want to try using the feelings formula to express them. Consider the following examples:

1. You're in the middle of the "battle for the remote."

Instead of saying, "Who made you king of the remote control?"

Try, "When you change the TV channel without asking me, I feel like what I want doesn't matter to you."

2. You're discussing finances and the conversation is "going south."

Instead of saying, "You spent *what* on a new camera? Are you crazy? What in the world were you thinking? Obviously, not about our budget!"

Try, "I'm really worried about how we will manage our money after marriage when you ignore our present budget by buying such an expensive camera."

3. You're upset when your partner forgets to call—again.

Instead of saying, "You never call me when you say you will—why would I want to marry someone so unreliable?"

Try, "I'm fearful of making a deeper commitment to you when time after time you say you're going to call me and then you forget."

Being able to express negative feelings in a positive way is important to a healthy relationship, but just as important is taking the time and effort to really listen to each other.

CONNECTING THROUGH LISTENING

You may know how to use the connecting pattern of communication and how to express your feelings, but if you don't listen, your communication will be lacking. Have you ever thought about why is it so hard to listen? Could it be that instead of really listening, we are thinking about what we want to say when the other stops talking? Listening is more than politely waiting for your turn to talk.

Listen, Don't React

In James 1:19 we read, "Everyone should be quick to listen, slow to speak and slow to become angry." Too often we get it backwards—we are slow to listen and very quick to speak and extremely quick to become angry! Yet what wisdom we find in this verse! Think about it. If first, we would really try to listen and to understand the other person, it wouldn't be so hard to back off and to avoid the confronting pattern. Why? Because we know that after listening to and seeking to understand our partner's perspective, we will get a chance to say what we want to say. And what we say will probably be more "connecting" because we took the time to listen and to try to understand the other person.

Another tip: Perhaps you have heard the old adage, "God gave us two ears and one mouth, so maybe we are supposed to listen twice as much as we talk." As we listen intently, we need to be aware of the total message.

Listen for the Total Message

It is not enough just to hear words. We need to hear the total message. Years ago Kodak did a study to determine what makes up "the total message" in communication. These are the results:

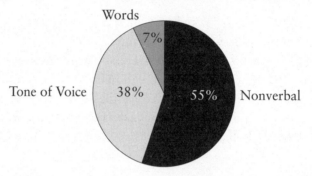

1. Our nonverbal communication accounts for 55 percent of the total message. This includes the shrugs, stares, and glares. Do you know "the look"? Or picture one person trying to talk as the other is glued to the newspaper or computer screen. Have you ever agreed with your partner but given another message in the disgust on your face? There is no colder place to be than with someone who is using the "right words" to gloss over bitterness, anger, and hostility.
2. Tone of voice accounts for 38 percent of the total message. This includes the sighs and nagging tones that creep into our conversations. Have you ever said, "Okay," when it really wasn't okay? Your tone of voice can send a completely different message.
3. The words actually spoken make up only 7 percent of the total message. The next time you talk to your partner, you may want to consider that your words are only a very small part of the true message.

We have found that if we really want to communicate and connect, we need to take time to listen. We need to listen with our heart and try to express our feelings in an appropriate way. We need to be willing to make a contract not to attack each other or defend ourselves. If you listen and make your own contract, you may find that you will be able to share your intimate feelings and work through the hard issues.

Communication is hard work. Even marriage educators don't always get it right. For instance, we (the Browns) recently used all three patterns of communication in one day!

HIKING IN THE ROCKIES

It was a beautiful fall day. We were caught up with the office work. Writing assignments were all done. It was time to play. Curt suggested we go golfing. I wasn't really in a golfing mood; instead, the Rockies in our backyard were calling. I convinced Curt that we should take a hike. Soon it would be too cold for long, leisurely hikes, and the trails would be covered with snow. We chattered away about the day and our soon-to-be outing in the Rockies. Pattern one communication was alive and well.

I picked out a short, easy, two-and-a-half mile hiking trail in the woods near Evergreen. We have a hiking trail guide and have embarked on a number of the hikes and have always found the directions easy to follow. But this hike would prove to be a different story. We were having a great conversation—really connecting—but not watching closely where we were going.

After about forty-five minutes we wandered off the main trail without realizing it. We got turned around and did some backtracking. We didn't want to admit it, but we were lost in the Colorado Rockies. An hour-long hike was going on two-and-a-half hours, and we had no idea where we were. Thunderclouds were forming in the sky in the distance and dusk was approaching. Both of us were getting a little fearful and very frustrated.

Curt stormed into the second pattern of communication, the confronting pattern. "Natelle, why did you pick this trail? Why not go on a path we already knew? We wouldn't be lost if you had agreed to go golfing! This is all your fault!"

I was not to be outdone. "Hey, you're the one with the perfect sense of direction. Really perfect, huh? Why couldn't you follow the trail signs? It's not my fault we're lost; it's yours!"

At one point, Curt hurried on ahead to look for a trail back to the car. I yelled for him and when he didn't answer, I wondered if he were so angry with me that he'd leave me in the woods, or if a bear had attacked him, or if a bear was going to attack me, or if it was going to storm and I would be struck by lightning.

Eventually, we reconnected and mutually agreed that we didn't want to be eaten by bears while we were upset and attacking each other. In the connecting pattern I said, "Curt, I'm sorry I yelled at you. I'm scared. I know that bears are still out, and we're lost and it's starting to get dark."

Curt admitted that he was also scared. But once we calmed down and reconnected, we came up with a plan. We would head toward the setting sun (fortunately, the storm clouds had moved on), which we thought would be toward the car—trail or no trail. That was the right choice, and in another hour or so we came to the clearing where our car was parked.

Our hike could have turned into a total disaster if we had let it. Fortunately, that time we chose to move from the confronting pattern to the connecting one—a smart move that may have saved our lives. On that day it did help to save our marriage harmony!

Now it's time to check your own communication. Turn to Date Three in the Dating Guide and get ready to talk and connect!

Date Four

Solving Problems as a Couple

Everyone should be quick to listen,
slow to speak and slow to become angry.
James 1:19

"No way, I am absolutely not moving to Wisconsin!" snapped Mindy. "I can't believe you are even bringing this up."

"You just don't get it, do you, Mindy?" Brent said. "I've got to move back home to help my parents. Why are you being so selfish about this?"

Mindy and Brent, an engaged couple who came for premarital help, are both serious and intense people. As the oldest sibling, Brent felt an obligation to return to Wisconsin to help his parents because his father's health was beginning to decline. Mindy had grown up in Illinois, and she had no desire to move back to the Midwest. She enjoyed her family and friends in Colorado, and her new career was off to a great start.

In regard to this important issue, Brent assumed Mindy didn't care about his father, and Mindy believed Brent wasn't considering her feelings. Their conversations about where to live and how best to help Brent's parents quickly escalated into full-blown arguments that left both feeling misunderstood, confused, and angry. They couldn't effectively discuss the problem, let alone begin to solve it.

Brent and Mindy aren't alone in their inability to solve problems. Most couples, from time to time, struggle to stay positive and resist attacking the other. We hate to admit it, but too often the ways we handle conflict can be compared to certain characteristics of some of the members of the animal kingdom.[1] Do you see yourself in these inappropriate methods?

HOW DO YOU HANDLE CONFLICT?

The Turtle—The Withdrawer

Dave is a turtle. When faced with conflict, his typical reaction is to withdraw. He just pulls his head inside his hard shell for the duration. Claudia, who occasionally likes a heated verbal exchange, can beat on his shell, but to no avail.

Are you a turtle? Do you usually withdraw from conflict? You may withdraw physically, like getting up and walking out of the room, or you may withdraw emotionally, by turning the other person off. Maybe you feel hopeless and that you can't win anyway, so why discuss it? The problem with withdrawing is that it hurts the relationship and prevents your finding a possible solution.

The Skunk—The Attacker

Do you identify with the skunk? The skunk is a master of sarcasm and is usually very quick verbally. He would rather make the other person look bad than deal with any personal shortcomings.

Claudia is like a skunk. Her natural tendency is to attack and make Dave stink. She would rather focus on what he did or didn't do and avoid any responsibility on her part.

Over the years of leading Marriage Alive seminars, we've met many turtles who are married to skunks. We've even observed a new breed— the *skurtle*. The skurtle, a combination of the skunk and the turtle, handles conflict by attacking the other person and then retreating into her shell!

The Chameleon—The Yielder

Natelle identifies with the chameleon. Years ago in her family of origin she learned to be a pleaser. The youngest of four sisters, she found it was dangerous to express her opinion—actually she wasn't allowed to have one. Even today she likes to please others but is now more assertive (occasionally she can even resemble a skunk).

The chameleon turns colors to blend into the environment, thus avoiding conflict. She agrees with whatever opinions are being expressed. When she is with a quiet group, she is quiet too. When she is with a loud group, she becomes loud. Her desire to fit in and be accepted prevents her from expressing her real opinion, so when she meets conflict, she'll go along with the crowd.

Often this is the person who suddenly leaves a marriage after years of "giving in." No one can understand what triggered his departure because he always adapted so convincingly. But everyone has a limit—like a balloon that stretches and stretches and then suddenly pops.

The Beaver—The Avoider

Curt is our resident beaver. If an emotional or heated issue comes up, sometimes instead of addressing the issue head on, Curt disappears to another part of the house, turns on the TV, or logs on to the Internet.

The beaver, when faced with conflict, gets busy. Often he is our workaholic, and when there's tension at home, he'll find an extra project to fill his time.

The Owl—The Intellectualizer

The owl, like the turtle, avoids conflict. His methods are just different. He is the intellectualizer; his motto is "Avoid feelings at all cost!" The owl gladly discusses an issue intellectually, but has no feelings from his cranium down. He likes to deal with facts and ideas.

The Gorilla—The Winner

The gorilla has to win at all costs. His favorite weapons are manipulation and intimidation. Underneath his tough skin is a person who may be very insecure and wants to look good no matter what the cost. He keeps files of old grudges, hurts, and wrongs to pull out and use at the appropriate time. He loves to tell you what is wrong with everything and why he is right!

We will never forget the seminar when one participant turned out to be the classic gorilla. Each session was a struggle because Tony constantly interrupted us to tell us what we were doing wrong—or how we could do it better "his way." He continually attacked and put down his partner. The solution came from among the participants. During a break, several participants slipped away and came back with a huge bunch of bananas for Tony, the gorilla. He finally got the message! Did he change drastically after that? Not really, but he worked on modifying his behavior.

What's Your Style?

Do you identify with any of our animal friends? You might want to think back to the last time you were angry. Do you remember how you felt? Did you feel misunderstood? Fearful? Frustrated? Let down? All alone? How did you respond?

When the turtle becomes angry, he tends to withdraw; the skunk tends to attack; the chameleon may yield; the beaver often gets busy; the owl usually intellectualizes; and the gorilla really wants to win.

Think about what would be an appropriate response to anger:

_____ *I could put the "hot potato" down and let it cool.*
_____ *I could get out of the confronting communication pattern quickly.*
_____ *I could stop the escalation of my anger.*
_____ *We could resolve the conflict together and move on into intimacy.*
_____ *Other*

The good news is that there is hope. All of the above positive responses are possible. But first it is important to deal with the anger and get out of the confronting pattern.

From our years of working with couples, we believe the key to resolving conflict isn't the thing you are arguing about; the key is developing a way to look at that issue from the same side. The authors of *Fighting for Your Marriage* encourage couples to work at resolving conflict as a team: "You have a choice when dealing with a problem. Either you will nurture a sense that you are working together against the problem, or you will operate as if you are working against each other."[2]

As we talked about on Date Three, developing expertise in expressing your true feelings and understanding those of your partner can help facilitate your working together as a team. We encourage you to keep on talking until you both understand the issue and desire a solution— even if you have to give a little or, even harder, give a lot. At this point, the steps for conflict resolution are a piece of cake! First let's talk about how to do the hard work of discussing the problem. Then we will suggest four simple steps for solving problems.

DISCUSSING PROBLEMS

Sometimes it is really hard to talk civilly about a problem. Actually, many of the issues we argue about aren't solvable or don't actually need a resolution, but we do need to be able to talk about them and understand each other's perspective.

Dr. John Gottman, marital researcher at the University of Washington, writes in his book, *The Seven Principles for Making Marriage Work,* "All marital conflicts, ranging from mundane annoyances to all-out wars, really fall into two categories: Either they can be resolved, or they are perpetual, which means they will be a part of your lives forever, in some form or another."[3]

Dr. Gottman reports that 69 percent of martial conflicts fall into the "perpetual problems" category, like the battle of the thermostat. At home, shivering Diana wants the thermostat set at 74° F and sweating Jim wants it set at 68° F. One of the two is virtually always too cold or too hot, depending upon who adjusted the thermostat last. In the car it's the same scenario. The thermostat issue is a perpetual, unsolvable problem that many couples grapple with.

Another couple, Drew and Amy, disagrees on how fast to drive. Amy faithfully abides by the speed limit; Drew is a speed demon. They continually tell each other to slow down or speed up! Or consider the couple who is continually fighting the toothpaste war. One likes to neatly roll the toothpaste tube; the other is a creative squeezer.

Dr. Gottman reports that despite their differences these couples can remain very satisfied with their marriages, if they can learn a way to deal with their issues so they don't overwhelm them. And it starts with identifying the problem and then discussing it productively and positively.

One Window at a Time, Please!

The first step is to talk about one issue at a time. In the past when we tried to discuss a sensitive issue, we often pulled in other issues, and before we knew it, we were more angry and upset with each other than when we first started our discussion.

We have found that discussing an issue is difficult to do when we get off the subject or attempt to address several issues at once. It reminds us of working in a Windows computer program. A feature of this program is that you can have several windows open at the same time. I (Claudia) tend to get carried away and open another window while the original window is open. Then I open another, then another, and so on. Before I know it, my computer is overloaded with open windows, and I see a little box that displays one of a number of unpleasant messages like, "You have performed an illegal operation." Then I see the dreaded blue screen, all the keys freeze up, and all I have is trouble!

The same thing happens when we try to bring up other issues in problem discussion. We have found that it is best to stick with one issue until we both understand how each other feels about it. We want to stay in the same window and not open other windows or we'll experience a communication crash.

Learning to Share the Floor

Fighting for Your Marriage gives us a grid for staying in one window at a time using the Speaker/Listener Technique, and encouraging couples to "share the floor."[4] Anything can be used to designate who has the floor. You can pick up a pencil, your glasses, or a glass and say, "I have the floor." The person with the floor is the speaker. The person without the floor is the listener. The goal is to discuss the issue, stay on topic, and get to the point where you both understand the other's feelings and viewpoint.

The Speaker/Listener Technique offers partners a safe way to talk about sensitive issues. It gives structure and enhances your ability to stay in one window and say clearly and understandably what you are feeling without attacking the other person. At first it may seem awkward, but the technique works because both people follow the rules. This technique is used when you need the structure—when you need help staying in one window. Here are the rules:

Rules for the Speaker

- Speak for yourself. Don't mind read!
- Keep statements brief. Don't go on and on.
- Stop to let the Listener paraphrase.

Rules for the Listener

- Paraphrase what you hear.
- Focus on the Speaker's message. Don't rebut.

Rules for Both

- The Speaker has the floor.
- Speaker keeps the floor while Listener paraphrases.
- Share the floor.

Before you try using the Speaker/Listener Technique, you may want to review the communications skills in Date Three.

1. Use the connecting pattern of communication and utilize the feelings formula.
2. Start your sentences with "I." Avoid "you" statements and "why" questions.
3. Agree not to verbally attack each other or verbally defend yourself.

Now let's go back to Mindy and Brent. They were stuck in an unproductive discussion of where they should live after they were married—Wisconsin to be near Brent's dad or Colorado to be close to Mindy's family and friends. The Speaker/Listener Technique gave them the safety and structure they needed to discuss their differences without fighting. Let's listen in on their discussion:

Brent (Speaker): As my dad's health continues to decline, I feel a need to return to Wisconsin to help my parents.

Mindy (Listener): You feel a sense of duty to help your parents because of your dad's poor health.

Brent (Speaker): Exactly. As the oldest sibling, I feel a sense of obligation. My brother is in the military, and my sister is in college, so it's impossible for them to help Mom and Dad right now.

Mindy (Listener): You don't think your brother or sister can help, so the responsibility falls on you.

Brent (Speaker): Mom can't take care of Dad and maintain the house and take care of necessary repairs. I would be helping her as well as him.

Mindy (Listener): Your mother as well as your father would benefit by your help.

(Brent hands Mindy the floor. Now Mindy becomes the Speaker.)

Mindy (Speaker): I love living in the Rocky Mountains of Colorado. I was born in the Midwest and have no desire to move back there.

Brent (Listener): You enjoy your life here in Colorado and want to stay here.

Mindy (Speaker): Yes, I am really close to my family here in Colorado. I also enjoy my friends and activities here.

Brent (Listener): Your family and friends are important to you, and you would miss them.

Mindy (Speaker): I'm afraid that if we move to Wisconsin, we'll never move back to Colorado.

Brent (Listener): You think that a move to Wisconsin would be permanent. (She hands him the floor).

Brent (Speaker): I had no idea you thought a move to Wisconsin would be permanent. I was thinking if we did move, it would be for only a couple years.

Mindy (Listener): You're thinking a temporary move, like for a couple years.

Brent (Speaker): Right. Also, I'm not saying we have to move now. I just want you to be open to the idea of moving if my dad's situation gets worse.

Mindy (Listener): I hear you saying that we might not need to move right after our wedding. You want me to be open to moving if your parents really need you.

Brent (Speaker): Yes, I think we're beginning to understand each other.

Mindy and Brent were doing a good job of staying on topic and were beginning to be able to validate each other. For the first time, they could see the other person's viewpoint.

Only use the Speaker/Listener Technique to discuss the problem; don't try to solve it. If you find yourself discussing possible solutions, stop and go back to problem discussion. Remember, many issues we argue about are perpetual, unsolvable problems, and we just need to be able to talk about them in an understanding way.

Once you have fully discussed the problem, and you both really understand each other's viewpoint, you can move on to solving the problem.

SOLVING PROBLEMS

Once feelings are expressed and understood, the issue is fully discussed, and you've both agreed on what the issue is and that you want a solution, consider the following four steps for resolving conflict.[5]

Step 1: *Restate the problem.* You may want to write it down.

Step 2: *Identify which of you feels the greatest need for a solution and the other person's contribution to the problem.*

Step 3: *Brainstorm possible solutions.* Brainstorming can be a creative process, so we encourage you to write down as many possible solutions as possible without evaluating them. While doing this you will find your list of potential solutions expanding. Using humor can also help.

Step 4: *Select a plan of action.* Your brainstorming suggestions most likely will fall into the following three areas.

- *Give a gift of love.* You could say, "This is just more important to you than it is to me at this time, so I'll choose to go along with what you want to do."

- *Give a gift of individuality.* We don't have to agree on everything. This just may be one of our perpetual issues (like temperature) we need to accept and go on with our life.

- *Give the gift of compromise.* We each can give a little and meet in the middle on this issue.

Now, let's go back to Mindy and Brent and see how they worked together through these four steps to solve the issue concerning how to care for Brent's parents.

Step 1: *Restate the problem.* Because Mindy and Brent had already defined the issue and discussed it, the first step was easy for them. They wrote, "We want to find a mutually agreeable plan for helping and supporting Brent's parents in a way that doesn't hurt our own relationship."

Step 2: *Identify which of you feels the great need for a solution and the other person's contribution to the problem.* Brent felt the most responsibility for supporting his parents. Mindy didn't want to relocate to Wisconsin and leave her family in Colorado.

Step 3: *Brainstorm possible solutions.* As Mindy and Brent brainstormed together, their list looked something like this:

1. Move to Wisconsin permanently.
2. Stay in Colorado.
3. Move to Wisconsin for two years; then move back to Colorado.
4. Move the parents to Colorado.
5. Check with siblings for their help.

6. Stay in Colorado but Brent will fly back every couple of months to check on his parents.

Step 4: *Select a plan of action.*

So what solution did Brent and Mindy find? As you may remember, earlier they did an excellent job of discussing the problem. Their diligence in talking it out helped them when they came to the point of actually choosing a plan of action.

For now, Brent and Mindy decided they will remain in Colorado. Brent will go back every six weeks for a long weekend. This allowed him to help both of his parents. Mindy was satisfied also because she can still live near her family, friends, and job. This plan of action seemed to meet both of their needs. In the future, they may need to revisit this issue, but for now they can move on to other issues.

EVERYBODY HAS PROBLEMS

As long as we are alive, we will face hard situations and have to make choices, so let us encourage you now before you say "I do" to learn the skills of problem discussion and problem solution. The dullest marriages on earth are the ones where both partners have decided to coexist and just tolerate one another. No conflict but no intimacy either. Let us challenge you to work hard at solving problems as a couple both now and in the future. Your marriage is worth it!

A Few Tips

As you deal with problems you might want to consider the following tips:

1. *Choose your timing wisely.* Avoid bringing up emotional issues late at night when you're tired, hungry, or already out of sorts.
2. *Avoid manipulation.* Manipulation destroys the relationship. It is not always easy, but it's worth the effort to work together to find honest resolution. Your marriage will be stronger for it.

3. *Consider who has the most expertise in the area you're discussing.* To us it just makes good sense to defer to the one with the most knowledge and experience in an area.

4. *Don't give up.* It is not always easy to discern what the best plan of action is. If your first choice doesn't work, try again.

If you just can't seem to work things out, try consulting your pastor, mentor, trusted friend, or counselor for some short-term help. If you're going down a one-way street in the wrong direction, you don't need a pedestrian shouting to you that you're going the wrong way. What you really need is a friendly police officer to come along, stop the traffic, and help you get turned around. That's what a counselor can do for you.

Most times, if you are willing to pull together, attack the problem and not each other, process anger, and do a good job of discussing the problem before you try to solve it, you will find a workable solution.

Now turn to Date Four in the Dating Guide and get ready for another great date. You too can learn to solve problems as a couple!

Date Five

Managing Your Money

To some people, money means power; to others, love.
For some, the topic is boorish,
in bad taste; for others, it's more private than sex.
Add family dynamics to the mix
and for many you have the subject from hell.
Karen Peterson, USA Today[1]

*N*eil, you're kidding, aren't you? You didn't actually spend $25 this week at Starbucks, did you?"

"Gosh, Rachel, relax. I just bought coffee!"

"But, Neil, $25 a week adds up to $100 a month and $1,200 a year! That's a lot of money. Think what we could do with that money if we saved it!"

Before marriage, Rachel and Neil kept their finances separate. After marriage, they agreed to combine their money and budget all their expenditures. Tracking every penny seemed crucial to penny-pinching Rachel, who grew up in a family that reused teabags. She felt that if Neil really loved her, he would save because that is the way to protect their future together.

Neil considered tracking pennies totally ridiculous. A free-wheeling spender, Neil grew up in a family who ate out almost every meal and where money seemed to grow on trees! He felt if Rachel really loved him, she would trust him to spend wisely because it would be an investment in their life together.

Who do you most identify with—Rachel or Neil? Now think about how your family approached financial issues. You may be surprised when you realize the basic attitudes about money that you are bringing into your marriage often come from your family of origin. Rachel didn't just decide to become a penny-pincher—she grew up in a family that daily reinforced saving and being frugal. On the other hand, in Neil's family, money was always available for whatever he really wanted. His philosophy is that if you need something, just buy it.

In some cases, instead of repeating the economic situation of the family of origin, some reject that model. Consider another couple, Ruth and Nathan, who have been seriously dating for two years and are considering getting engaged. Ruth grew up in a very frugal family and promised herself that if she ever had money she would spend it freely. As a highly paid ad executive, she enjoys an affluent lifestyle. Nathan is a saver. Both couples, Ruth and Nathan and Rachel and Neil, will need to come to grips with how they are going to manage their finances when they marry. If they ignore talking about finances before marriage, conflict over finances will possibly erupt soon after they marry.

MONEY PROBLEMS UP AHEAD

For couples marrying today, how to handle finances is a huge issue. In the past many couples married in their early twenties and most didn't have a financial identity until after marriage. Today, couples are marrying later and often, like Ruth, have already established their career and 401k accounts, plus have their own credit cards (often with accompanying debt) and college loans—all in their individual names. They are used to controlling and managing their own money.

Also if you are marrying later in life or if this is a second marriage, you may be bringing valuable assets into the new relationship. It is critical that couples talk about finances *before* they marry so they have a complete understanding of what each is bringing into the relationship.

Perhaps you have already established a pattern of handling finances together, and you assume your way will work after you marry. But for couples in the first five years of marriage, financial issues appear as top problematic issues for every group, and this includes couples who had already merged their finances before marriage.[2]

David Olson, founder of the PREPARE Premarital Inventory and coauthor of *Empowering Couples*, concurs that "financial issues are the most common source of stress for couples and families. Historically, economics was an important reason for marriage, whereas today finances are a common reason cited for divorce."[3]

TWO DANGER SIGNS — DEBT BEFORE AND AFTER YOU SAY "I DO"

Two months into their engagement, Lori discovered that her fiancé Dan had more than $18,000 in credit card debt! She exploded, "Dan, why didn't you tell me about your debt before now? How could you have done this? I thought you were more responsible than that! I'm not sure I want to go on with the wedding plans! How can I ever trust you again?"

Even though the wedding date had been set, Lori immediately broke the engagement until Dan addressed the debt issue. Others simply take their debt into their marriage, adding to the problems they will be facing in the first year of marriage.

Fortunately, Lori and Dan's story had a happy ending. Dan consulted a financial adviser and with his help was able to establish a workable plan for reducing his credit card debt. After he followed this plan for making consistent payments for several months, he and Lori reset their wedding date, but they pushed the date out far enough to make sure his credit card debt was well under control before saying "I do." They also worked on establishing a workable budget for the first year of their marriage.

More "Before Marriage" Debt

While Lori and Dan's credit problems were moderate, Tara and Sean's were more severe. Before marriage they had almost $37,000 in credit card debt between the two of them. In addition, Tara had $15,000 in student loans that she needed to begin repaying. They needed help— more than this date would give them!

They took the first step by getting free assistance from the Consumer Credit Counseling Services to decide on a budget and a plan to consolidate their debt and were making great progress until they booked their European honeymoon with plastic!

Unfortunately these two couples are not the exception. According to the book, *You Paid How Much for That*, "The average household has more than $8000 on credit cards. More than 1.2 million people went bankrupt in 2000, and it is estimated that by the year 2005 more than 3 million bankruptcies will be filed annually. More than 70% of Americans report they live from pay check to pay check. Many indicate they are constantly worried they will not be able to pay their bills. In fact, many couples are actually living on their credit cards rather than on their current income."[4]

Debt After You Say "I Do"

While one financial danger sign is debt brought into the marriage, a second danger sign is escalating debt in the first few years of marriage.

Cammie and Keith met in college and both avoided college loans by co-oping and working part time. When they married, everyone thought they had their financial feet on the ground and soon would be sitting on "easy street." Both had entry level jobs.

They lived in a modest apartment with low rent but soon grew dissatisfied with their living arrangements. All their friends were buying houses, and they reasoned if they bought a house they wouldn't be throwing away money each month for rent. But as they began to look at the housing market, they discovered what they really wanted was more expensive than they had thought it would be.

Then they found the house of their dreams. "It's an investment," they reasoned and somehow talked themselves into committing almost 50 percent of their net monthly income after taxes and tithe for house payments. Soon the financial pressures spilled over into their relationship. Both were trying to put in overtime at work to help pay the bills and what time they had together they were exhausted and irritable, which often led to heated arguments.

Cammie and Keith needed help. First, they needed to answer some hard questions about their value system and financial goals. Then they needed some practical help budgeting.

FOUR STEPS FOR MANAGING YOUR MONEY

If these three couples had developed a practical financial plan, they could have avoided some of their current financial problems. To help you get off on a positive start, we suggest the following four action steps: evaluate your present debt, define your financial goals carefully, develop a workable budget, and manage and monitor your money. If you follow these steps, you can make great progress in managing your money—even before you say "I do."

Step 1: Evaluate Your Present Debt

The first step is look closely at your present debt level by using the following chart. You may want to do a chart for each of you and then combine them to get a true picture of the debt you are bringing into your marriage.

Loans/Existing Debt	Amount	Rate	Payment
Credit Card	_____	___	_____
	_____	___	_____
	_____	___	_____
Car Loans	_____	___	_____
Student Loans	_____	___	_____
	_____	___	_____
Other Loans	_____	___	_____
TOTAL	_____	TOTAL	_____

Now that you have the numbers down in black and white, what do they tell you? If you both feel comfortable with the debt load, great. If one or both of you have concerns, you may want to discuss how you think debt may affect your relationship. For many couples considering marriage, credit card debt and student loans are huge obstacles. Interest on the debt can be a real killer for long-term financial goals. The main economic danger of debt is that the interest keeps compounding, which works against you. Financial pressures can strain your relationship, so you may want to discuss this now.

What steps can you take to begin to reduce your debt level? If you are paying a high interest rate on a loan, consider refinancing with a lower interest rate to lower your monthly payments. Do you have money sitting in a money market account earning a low interest rate? Maybe this money could be used to pay off a loan.

If you are driving an expensive car, you might consider selling it and purchasing a less expensive car. Some choose to refinance a loan with a longer term to lower the monthly payment, but this can be risky because you may end up paying a lot more in interest. You need a realistic plan to repay the loan, not just a hope that your income will increase. A financial advisor can provide sound advice for your situation. What is most important is that the two of you discuss and evaluate your present debt.

Step 2: Define Your Financial Goals

Whatever your approach to handling your finances and debts, it helps to have well-defined financial goals—goals that you mutually agree on. In setting financial goals and working to achieve them, let us add one caution: It is possible to end up with all the things we would like to have, but no time to enjoy them. We can have it all and actually have nothing.

M. Scott Peck, in *The Road Less Traveled,* writes that a sign of maturity is the ability to delay gratification.[5] Yet we live in an instant world—instant oatmeal, instant coffee, and instant credit. Continually we hear that we can have it all and have it right now. If you are bored and have the right credit card, you can whisk your honey off to a romantic island—no need to even pack. We are told to "Just do it!" Many problems in marriage could be lessened if we learn to delay gratification!

Perhaps we need to learn to live with less. Living without something you never have had is not a sacrifice. Without the constant bombardment of advertisements and television commercials, many things we desire we wouldn't even know about!

Another issue in defining your financial goals deals with career choices. Are you entering marriage with both of you dedicated to your careers? Dual careers do not have to become a duel—not if you take the time to talk about them before you marry. A majority of couples entering marriage today will both have income-producing jobs, and this will affect so many areas of living: household responsibilities, financial decisions, where to live, parenting children, and so on. When and if children come along, should one of the spouses put their career on hold to take care of the baby?

If you are career-driven, how will the time away at work affect your relationship with your future spouse and the time you will have for one another? Should the couple move for the benefit of one's career?

Barbara Markey, founder of the FOCCUS Premarital Inventory, points out that another consideration is that many young adults do not have patterns from their family of origin on how to manage a dual career marriage. The current generation is being required to "write the book" on building strong marriages with the variables involved in dual careers.[6]

Plus, some have grown up with opposite models. As I (Natelle) shared earlier, I grew up in a family when both of my parents pursued careers, so as Curt and I were planning to get married, I was also considering how to launch my own career in business. In fact, the job market was so tight, I thought it made sense to be flexible. Whoever found a job first was fine with me.

Curt, however, had a completely different perspective. Dual careers were nowhere on his radar screen. We had to work through the issue of whether both of us should pursue careers. If so, who would take the lead responsibility when children came along?

Step 3: Develop a Workable Financial Plan

The first part of a workable financial plan is to track how you are spending money. You will want to track both large and small expenditures. How often have you come to the end of the month and asked yourself, "Where did all my money go?" Besides meeting your current needs, budgeting helps with your financial goals. Before you establish a budget, it might be helpful to record your actual expenses. Tracking how you both spend money for the next month or two (even before you marry) may help you to understand your present spending patterns.

Also consider expenses you may pay every six months such as property taxes or car and life insurance. After you track how you are spending money, then you probably will make some adjustments. See the sample worksheet on the next page.

Your financial plan will need to be updated as your financial situation changes. Creating a spending plan is extra work, but the results will be worth it.

Like many other young couples, Nick and Amy struggled consistently with their finances. Then they decided to really watch how they spent their money. The results? After several months of closely tracking their money, they began to save $500 per month. Nick and Amy were thrilled with their new financial position.

For more help in this area, please refer to Helpful Resources on page 141 for suggested resources to help you in developing a workable financial plan.

Financial Plan Worksheet

Income (after taxes)	Monthly Total
Hers_____	
His_____	
Other_____	_____
Rent or house payment	_____
Utilities	_____
Groceries and household expenses	_____
Phone (land line and cell phone)	_____
Insurance (life, health, home, car, etc.)	_____
Car (gas and repairs)	_____
Loan repayments	_____
Medical expenses	_____
Clothing	_____
Eating out	_____
Gifts and entertainment	_____
Donations	_____
Other expenses _____	_____
_____	_____
_____	_____
TOTAL INCOME_____	
TOTAL EXPENSES	_____
NET DIFFERENCE	_____

Step 4: Manage and Monitor Your Money

"How are we going to handle our money once we are married?" is an important question to consider. If you have already merged your money, you may feel you have it all figured out—but the system you're using now may not continue to work as well in the closeness of a marriage relationship.

The basic question after marriage is, "Will it be yours, mine, or ours?" Let us (the Arps) share with you three ways over the years of our marriage we have handled money. Please note that you don't have to choose one way to handle money for the rest of your life. One way may be best when you are just starting your married life and another way may work better when you have children or different jobs and so on.

The One-Pot Method

The first way we handled our money was to dump it all in one pot. We had one bank account. This worked great for us when we first started out and were on a very limited budget. We had so little money to manage! With one account we only had to pay one bank fee and only had one checking account to balance.

After we graduated from college, we still preferred having one bank account, but we graduated to having two checkbooks. This required that we keep very accurate records and compare checkbooks almost on a daily basis. The down side to this approach was that, with two checkbooks, at any given moment we didn't always know the balance of our account.

Pros and Cons for Newlyweds

Pros: This method can work well if both agree on how money should be spent and how much should be saved. Also it's easier to keep up with one bank account rather than two or more bank accounts.

Cons: If partners have very different ways of spending and handling money, this method can be problematic. If one person's income is much larger than the other, that one may feel he or she is contributing unfairly to the one pot.

The Two-Pot Method (Separate Accounts, Joint Payments)

When the one-pot method no longer met our needs, we changed to the separate accounts, joint payments method. We each had separate accounts, and we each were responsible for certain expenses—Claudia kept up with groceries, cleaning supplies, dry cleaning, purchasing clothes, and so on. Dave paid the regular monthly expenses and house payment.

At this time we only had one income, so according to our budget a certain amount of money went into Claudia's account. Actually we kept both names on each account so we didn't feel like it was "his" money or "her" money. This method worked well for us because we didn't have to keep up with everything—we each had our areas of financial responsibility. We did have to communicate and work together on our overall budget. On the con side, again, at any given time, we didn't always know the exact status of our finances.

Pros and Cons for Newlyweds

Pros: This approach to financial accountability gives a number of options. You can divide categories of expenses like we did, or you can pay equally out of your own accounts for set expenses. If you both are working and have lived on your own for years, you may like the feeling of independence and not having to be concerned about what the other might think of a purchase you made.

Cons: Because you really don't have to combine your monies, you may not work out a combined financial plan or budget. If one earns more than the other, one may feel taken advantage of, or if one earns less than the other, one may have little money left over for personal expenditures after paying expenses. Another option would be for each to contribute to expenses based on a percentage of the amount each earns.

The Three-Pot Method (Joint and Separate Accounts)

A third option is to each have a separate account and together have a joint account. We have also tried this method. From the joint account we paid major living expenses and also funded our IRA and savings accounts. Then we each had a separate account for our own discretionary spending and day-to-day expenses. For instance, Claudia's account also covered groceries and clothing.

Pros and Cons for Newlyweds

Pros: This method can be a compromise arrangement allowing you to function both independently as well as interdependently.

Cons: The more accounts you get, the harder it is to track them and the more time it takes for bookkeeping.

Newlyweds Sarah, a first-year school teacher, and Tim, an account executive, chose the three-pot method.

"In the beginning," Sarah said, "Tim and I really struggled with deciding how to handle our finances. Tim made so much more than I did, and there was considerable disparity between our two incomes."

Tim continued. "So we decided to pool all of our income into one joint account. From this account we pay household expenditures, car and student loans. It didn't bother me that I made more income than Sarah—but she still wanted to feel like she had some money of her own, so from our joint account we each took out an equal dollar amount to deposit into separate individual accounts."

Sarah and Tim could spend or save the money that was in their individual account for whatever purpose they determined. The three-pot method is working for them.

One Method Doesn't Work for All

No one way of handling finances is the right way for every couple. How you feel about money and the managing of it is very individualistic. Also, at different stages of marriage you may handle your finances in a number of different ways. The real concern is not how many bank accounts you have (separate or joint) or even how much money you have, but that you have a realistic and workable financial plan that you both agree on.

Financial Tips for Newlyweds

Following are several suggestions of ways to keep a handle on your finances. You may want to consider adopting the ones that are helpful for you:

1. *From time to time keep a record of each penny you spend.* One or two months of this will help you evaluate where your money is going and to modify spending and saving patterns, which is not so easy, but possible.

2. *Limit credit card spending to what you can pay off each month.* If things are really tight, we try not to use credit cards. Somehow, it's easier to justify buying with a credit card. We sometimes say, "Well, I'll probably bring it back, and it'll be easier to return if I charge it." It will be easier to buy, but a month later the bills arrive.

3. *Don't overlook the joy of giving.* Several couples we know also have a special bank account from which they give to their favorite causes. Each month they put money in that account, and from it they support their church, missionaries, and other ministries.

4. *Develop the habit of saving.* We used to say we just couldn't afford to save. The truth is we can't afford not to save. How

much we save is not as critical as developing the habit of saving. Consider long-term goals—such as retirement or educational goals. Also you may want to consider short-term goals such as a vacation for two at the beach.

LIFE INVOLVES CHOICES

Let's return to Cammie and Keith and their large house payments. The financial pressure of huge mortgage payments began to tear at the foundation of their relationship. Their situation was really impossible with such high fixed expenses. Costs could only be lowered so much, and their large house payment was a fixed cost that couldn't be lowered. Cammie and Keith did a lot of soul searching and talking and came to the conclusion their relationship was more important than living in a big, fancy house. They sold their large house and bought a smaller, more affordable home. Fortunately, they realized what they valued most before the financial pressures choked the life out of their marriage.

And what happened to Neil and Rachel who had such different spending styles? They made the decision together to work out a financial plan and conscientiously stick to it. For two months they tracked every penny spent. In fact, they took budgeting so seriously that they entered every penny into a spreadsheet at the end of each day. This made them realize they were spending about $2,000 per year on their dogs. Since their dogs are very precious to them, they decided to cut expenses elsewhere. They found that cutting costs was much easier than trying to increase their income. The first month on their new budget they saved $300, something Neil and Rachel had never done before, and they were ecstatic.

If Rachel and Neil and Cammie and Keith can make hard financial decisions, you can as well. You may want to take some time now before you say "I do" to talk about managing your money—it will be a wise investment in your future!

Now turn to Date Five in the Dating Guide and get ready for a date that will be a great investment in your financial future together!

Date Six

Leaving and Cleaving

Therefore shall a man leave his father and his mother,
and shall cleave unto his wife: and they shall be one flesh.
Genesis 2:24 KJV

A son is a son till he takes a wife, but a daughter is a daughter all of her life!"

So the saying goes. Not the best perspective if you want to have a successful marriage. Yet many parents of soon-to-be-wed daughters (and some sons) take this saying literally.

Shanna's mother said to her fiancé, "Jeremy, I will give you my blessings and permission to marry my daughter under one condition."

"What is that?" Jeremy asked.

"Every Christmas—no exceptions—you and Shanna will spend the holidays here with me."

If you were Jeremy, how would you respond? Little is written about healthy in-law relationships. Some say it's an oxymoron. Yet building a great marriage is easier when you have supportive parents and parents-in-law. Perhaps you are wondering what can be done *before* marriage to facilitate positive in-law relationships. The best advice we have is to become very familiar with the principles in Genesis 2:24 where we are told to leave mother and father and cleave to our spouse.

Based on this good advice we have two suggestions. First, share with each other your family history—how you grew up and what your past and present relationship is with your parents, siblings, and extended family. Second, be clear with your own parents about what you expect your relationship to look like after you are married. It will be helpful if you can reassure them of your love and respect, but they need to know that your first allegiance will be to your spouse!

LEAVING FAMILIES — HIS AND HERS

Have you considered that when you marry, you will be bringing together two unique family histories—two distinct personalities, two differing ways of looking at life? Into your marriage you will bring collections of qualities, attitudes, and gifts you received from your parents, siblings, aunts, uncles, grandparents, and cousins.

Consider that your expectations and your way of thinking and acting may be different from your partner's. Your communication and negotiation styles may be miles apart. All of these factors are greatly influenced by your family of origin. One task of newlyweds is to blend their lives together so they will have a style uniquely their own.

Getting to Know You—and Your Family!

How much do you know about each other's growing-up years? Many times couples assume that they know each other quite well and expect no surprises, yet each brings habits to the marriage that the other may not be aware of. Les and Leslie Parrott share a wonderful story from their newlywed days about their different approaches to serving catsup. Les grew up in a family where his mom always served catsup in a little dish—never in the bottle. Leslie's family simply put the bottle on the table. This seems like a very small issue, but for Les and Leslie in the early days of their marriage, it was an issue just the same!

After marriage, you may be surprised by many of your partner's small habits and ways of doing things—patterns picked up in his or her family of origin. On this date we suggest that you look at some of the patterns you picked up in your family of origin and talk about whether you need to make some adjustments in shaping your marriage. Following are some questions that marital pioneers David and Vera Mace suggest you ask each other *before* the wedding![1]

Questions to Ask Before the Wedding

1. What were your eating habits? Did you all sit down and eat together? Did you begin by saying grace? Who set the table? Who prepared the meal? Were mealtimes social times when your family connected? Who talked most during meals and about what? Who cleared the table and washed the dishes?

2. Did you share in the house cleaning? Were you required to do special jobs in the home? Did you get paid for helping with the housework?

3. How did your parents discipline you? Did you accept or rebel against this? Did you feel that your family rules were fair or unjust? Did you get fair treatment compared with others in the family?

4. How would you rate your parents' marriage? Were they loving and affectionate? Did they argue with each other? Were they good role models for your future marriage?

5. How did your parents teach you to manage money? Did you receive a regular allowance? Did you have the opportunity to earn what you needed? Did you save for special things you wanted? Did you have a bank account or credit card of your own? Did your parents have debts?

6. Can you remember your parents going through a crisis of any kind in their marriage? What happened and how did you feel about it?

7. What was your relationship with your siblings? Were you closer to one sibling? Were you an only child? If so, how did you feel about being an only child?

8. What did your parents teach you about sex? Did they make any rules for you about sexual behavior?

9. Do your parents approve of your choice of a marriage partner? Does your partner get along well with your parents?

10. What was your relationship with your grandparents? Did you know them well, and did they treat you kindly? What about aunts, uncles, cousins, and other relatives? Did you have close relationships with any of them?

11. Overall, how would you rate your family of origin on a scale of 1 to 10? How would you rate the family of your future spouse? Would your ratings be in agreement with your partner's ratings?

You might want to consider how your family of origin has shaped the way you approach and behave in close relationships. Can you see ways your living patterns harmonize with your partner's family history? Do you see ways your previous living patterns might clash? Into your marriage you will be bringing two separate histories, and your challenge is to blend your lives together and form a new pattern for your marriage. How to do this without interference from your parents and in-laws is a question we are often asked.

Advice Worth Taking

In their book *When the Honeymoon's Over,* the Maces give this sage advice: "There is one golden rule that all married couples should try earnestly to follow in their relationship to their families of origin. It is: *Try never to allow your family members, or any one of them, to make critical judgments of your marriage, or of your marriage partner, when your partner is not present to hear what is said.*"

The Maces continue, "When this happens, it nearly always causes trouble. Make it clear that you are open to receive helpful suggestions about how to improve your marriage relationship, because that will always be welcome. But you and your partner want to hear such suggestions together, so that you can, if necessary, act on them together.

"If suggestions about your behavior are, in fact, made by family members on either side to both of you together, always try to treat them seriously. If they seem not to be relevant, nevertheless take the trouble to explain carefully, and positively, why they are not acceptable."[2]

We encourage you to go the extra mile to develop healthy relationships with both sets of parents and to make every effort to promote mutual understanding. Your marriage will really benefit from support from your families of origin, so consider what you can do to foster healthy intergenerational relationships. A guiding principle in relating to family is to put your marriage first.

Let Parents Stand Beside, Not Between!

At a recent wedding, the unique presentation of the couple by both sets of parents impressed us. It went something like this:

> *Celebrant: The union of this couple brings together two family traditions, two systems of roots, in the hope that a new family tree may become strong and fruitful. Theirs is a personal choice and a decision for which they are primarily responsible. Yet their life will be enriched by the support of the families from which each comes. Will you, parents, encourage this couple in their marriage?*

Parents: We will.

Celebrant: Do you celebrate with them the decision they have made to choose each other?

Parents: We do.

Celebrant: Will you continue to stand beside them, yet not between?

Parents: We will.

This principle of realigning your priorities also appears in the traditional wedding choreography when the parents present the bride and step back from between her and the groom, joining their hands.

Sometimes it is hard for parents to step back and not give advice and interfere. As parents of married children, we realize how difficult this can be, but you can help your parents by being firm, yet loving. Sometimes, it is the couples themselves who are reluctant to cut the apron strings.

From day one Randy and Angela struggled with in-law relationships. For instance, Randy didn't understand why Angela objected to his Wednesday night out with his two brothers. And Randy was ticked with all the time Angela spent on the phone with her mom each evening after dinner. Isn't that supposed to be their time? Also he resented the fact that Angela discussed their marital problems with her mother.

We talked with Randy and Angela about how they needed to reevaluate their marital priorities and make some adjustments. It is easy to drift into marriage and slip into patterns passed down by your parents and grandparents. Randy's dad always had his night out, and Angela's mom checked in daily with her mom. But things weren't working well for Randy and Angela. They were both irritated. We suggested they talk about how to adjust their priorities so they both knew the other came first—before their parents, siblings, or friends. This concept is foundational for building a healthy, biblical marriage.

"For This Cause a Man Shall Leave His Father and Mother"

The foundation for marriage goes back many, many years and is recorded at the beginning of the first book of the Old Testament. In Genesis 2:24 we read, "For this reason a man will leave his father and mother and be united (cleave) to his wife, and they will become one flesh."

From this passage, we draw three marital principles that have helped us to keep our marriage growing and healthy and in-law relationships in their proper place: leaving, cleaving, and becoming one. On this date we will consider the first two principles, and on Date Seven we will look at the third one.

This verse describes leaving in the context of leaving your family of origin and forming your own family unit. It is more than physically leaving our parents' home—it is also reprioritizing our allegiance from our parents to our partner.

The "leaving" principle is obviously much more complicated to live out when couples live in the same house as or close to their parents. Recently we talked with Beth and Jonathan, who were soon to be married and who planned to live for a year with Jonathan's parents. Jonathan had one more year of college, and living together with his parents would help them out financially. How did Beth feel about this arrangement? While she thinks Jonathan's parents are great, we could sense some apprehension. Clearly, it would be harder for Jonathan to "leave his parents" if they are living under the same roof.

We advised them to live with less and find a small apartment near the university. In some circumstances it is necessary for several generations to live together because of limited resources. But Jonathan and Beth may find refocusing on each other and making other people and things a lower priority than each other more difficult to do if they are living with his parents.

After we completed our college degrees, we (the Arps) spent two years in Germany with the U.S. military. We were thousands of miles away from our parents and as much as we loved our family, we really benefited from this time apart. We had the opportunity to blend our two living patterns, to work out our own problems, and to develop our own style of marriage.

Rusty and Kiley weren't so lucky. They came to us in a last ditch effort to save their marriage. As they told us their story, it was obvious they had violated the basic principle of leaving. Rusty was still so emotionally attached to his mom and brothers that Kiley was convinced he loved them more than he loved her. When Rusty had choices as to how to spend his time, he chose his mom and brothers instead of Kiley. Holidays had to be celebrated with his family.

While Rusty's relationship with his family was a big issue, it didn't stop there. Rusty put his job, his friends, and his interests before his relationship with Kiley, and he wasn't willing to change. Sadly, their marriage didn't make it.

What about Unspoken Family Expectations?

No matter what time of year it is, holidays and special occasions seem to be approaching. What are your family's expectations? What are your partner's family's expectations? Misunderstandings arise when expectations are unspoken. During the first few years we (the Browns) were married, Curt's parents expected us to visit frequently since we lived less than an hour away. They assumed we would celebrate holidays with them at their home. No invitation necessary. When we didn't show up often enough, they complained that we never came to see them. I became confused and frustrated. If they wanted us to come, why didn't they call and invite us? After all, I didn't want them to show up on our doorstep uninvited and without warning. We didn't know what the expectations were until we missed fulfilling them.

Do you agree on which traditions and customs you will bring to your marriage? You may want to consider which traditions and holidays are special to each of you. Is there a way you can compromise and still stay connected with your family?

Remember, you need to creatively leave other things as less important and focus on each other. It's a choice you must make if you want your marriage to have a strong foundation.

BLENDING FRIENDSHIPS AND MARRIAGE

The principle of leaving also relates to relationships with friends. Your friends will affect your marriage, so on this date you'll have the opportunity to talk about how you will relate to your friends after you are married.

Kim, who is engaged to Scott, is concerned about the time he spends with friends of the opposite sex. She feels threatened, especially by his ex-girlfriends. Although Scott claims he no longer has any romantic inclinations, he still calls them to discuss work and mutual interests and friends. He can't understand why Kim is jealous.

They were spinning their wheels until they decided to try talking about Scott's friends using the Speaker/Listener Technique they learned on Date Three. Let's listen in on their conversation.

Kim (Speaker): Scott, I don't like you calling former girlfriends. Sometimes I wonder if you still have feelings for them.

Scott (Listener): You don't want me to call my friends. You think I'm still interested in them.

Kim (Speaker): It's okay to call friends; it's your former girlfriends that bother me. I wish you would talk to me instead of talking to them. I feel like I don't count.

Scott (Listener): You want me to talk to you, not to them. You feel discounted.

Kim (Speaker): Right. (Kim hands Scott the floor.)

Scott (Speaker): I didn't know that you were upset about this. To me, they are just friends, nothing more.

Kim (Listener): You consider them just friends, and you didn't realize that this is upsetting to me.

Scott (Speaker): I don't want you to feel threatened or jealous. If you feel that way, I'm sorry and I'll quit calling them.

Kim (Listener): You're going to quit calling them because you don't want me to feel threatened and jealous. (Scott hands Kim the floor.)

Kim (Speaker): Thanks, Scott, for considering my feelings. I feel better.

Scott (Listener): You feel better. So do I!

Kim told Scott how she felt—that she needed to know she was Scott's confidant. When Scott realized how Kim felt, he was willing to change his behavior and quit calling his former girlfriends because Kim was his highest priority.

But I Don't Like Your Friends!

What about when you don't like your partner's friends? Do you just have to tolerate them?

Nicole and Randy were seriously considering marriage. However, tension mounted whenever Randy asked Nicole to join him and his buddies (with their girlfriends) for an evening. Nicole simply didn't have anything in common with Randy's friends' girlfriends. She found their conversations shallow, catty, and boring. Consequently, when they were with Randy's buddies and their girlfriends, Nicole didn't enjoy herself.

After discussing this issue, Nicole and Randy agreed that sometimes Nicole would give Randy a gift of love and accompany him to special occasions such as birthday parties. Other times, Randy would hang out with his friends, and Nicole would stay home. They also agreed to develop new friendships with couples they could mutually enjoy.

Educating Your Single Friends

Prior to marriage, Jason divided his leisure time between mountain biking, lifting weights with his buddies at the fitness club, and hiking with his fiancée, Heather. After marriage, Jason and Heather wanted more couple time together, so Heather carved out time to jump on her bike and go to the fitness club with Jason. They are happy doing these things together; however, Jason's single friends just don't seem to get it. They call and don't understand why every time they call, Jason doesn't want to rush over to the fitness club to spot them. Jason has changed his friendship priorities and Heather is his top priority! Jason has to educate his friends; he doesn't want to drop them, but they need to realize that because he is now married, Heather comes first.

Building Mutual Friends

Do you already have friends in common? If not, we encourage you to pursue building some. Having couple friendships will enhance your own friendship and will be good for your marriage.

If you don't have strong couple friendships, then consider joining some groups where you would meet other couples who have similar values and interests. Consider joining a couples' Bible study or signing up for a community program or volunteering your time for a charity or ministry. Maybe you would like to take a course at the community college together or join a health club. You can build your own friendship while meeting other couples with similar interests.

CLEAVING TO ONE ANOTHER

When you successfully process leaving your parents and blending friends, you can then follow the second principle in Genesis 2:24: cleaving. When you cleave to one another, you build your own friendship and will naturally encourage one another. Cleaving gives a picture of commitment that goes beyond just sticking together. In *The Heart of*

Commitment, Scott Stanley, Ph.D., talks about the difference between sticking together and getting stuck. When you choose to cleave to each other, you're going beyond just being stuck—you're committing yourself to grow in intimacy—being that one person the other can always count on, sharing life on the deepest, most intimate level.[3]

Daily we have opportunities to apply the cleaving principle to our relationship. The daily pressures of life, the hard times as well as the good times, can help to glue us together. The key is to pull together instead of push apart. Consider what tends to pull you together. Kari and Keith enjoy cooking together. Susan and Rob are avid hikers and find that is their best time for deep conversations. Activities that create closeness are the things you want to do as often as possible.

Now think about what tends to put distance in your relationship. Those are the things you want to avoid. For us, when we get overcommitted and stressed, we react to each other. We snap at each other. We are short-tempered. We get impatient. So, as much as possible, we need to guard our schedules and avoid overcommitment. When you have a choice to make, you might ask yourself, "Will this bring us closer together, or will it put distance in our relationship?"

No one wants a mediocre marriage, but cleaving requires self-sacrifice. It calls for thinking of the other person and looking for ways to serve each other. It means being each other's best friend. What are you doing to build your friendship with your partner? Do you share common interests and hobbies? In a growing, healthy marriage, partners are continually looking for ways to cleave to one another—to encourage one another. Here are three suggestions for doing just that: focus on the positive, learn to laugh, and date your mate.

Focus on the Positive

Before marriage it is easy to focus on the positive. But once married, rose-colored glasses may begin to fade. You may discover that the person you think is just about perfect before marriage has some irritating habits after marriage. Johann Wolfgang von Goethe, the great German poet and philosopher, gave some good advice when he said, "If you treat a man as he is, he will stay as he is. If you treat him as if he were what he ought to be and could be, he will become that bigger and better man." We suggest looking at your partner through Goethe's eyes. Maybe your partner is in the process of taking a risk. Perhaps she is learning a new skill or even making a career change. Why not acknowledge and affirm your partner's strengths and desires to grow and change?

Ways to Focus on the Positive

Concentrate on each other's strengths.

As we observed on Date Two, everyone has strengths and weaknesses. Strengths and weaknesses assure us of neither success nor failure. They are merely the setting where we play out our marriage. Let each other operate out of your areas of strength. Even in weak areas, we can learn from each other.

Track your positives and negatives.

Dr. Gottman, in his book *Why Marriages Succeed or Fail,* says: "You must have at least five times as many positive as negative moments together if your marriage is to be stable."[4] For the next twenty-four hours, why not try to keep track of the number of positive to negative statements? Remember five to one is just staying even. Seven to one is a healthier ratio.

Make a positive list.

When we think negatively, it is easy to express our negative thoughts, but when we do have positive, tender thoughts, often we keep them to ourselves. Many years ago the apostle Paul encouraged the people at Philippi to think about what was positive instead of what was negative. In Philippians 4:8 we read, "Finally, brothers, whatever is true, whatever is noble, whatever is right, whatever is pure, whatever is lovely, whatever is admirable—if anything is excellent or praiseworthy—think about such things."

Don't we often do just the opposite? Whatever is untrue, whatever is wrong or whatever is negative, whatever is weak, those are the things we dwell on. Positive thoughts are worth developing. However, developing the habit of thinking positively takes time and persistence, so be prepared to persevere. You may want to think about your partner and make your own list. Can you think about one thing that is true about him? Does he demonstrate his love and commitment to you? How? What is one thing that is honorable? Perhaps he shows integrity in business and financial affairs. Then you could continue through the verse, considering how your partner is right, pure, lovely, and admirable.

When you feel yourself becoming negative, you may want to pull out your list and dwell on the other's positive qualities. Does your partner know how much you love and appreciate her? Why not take those positive thoughts and turn them into verbal affirmation? Our friend Carter made a list of thirty-one things he appreciated about his wife, Lindsey. He typed them, cut them up, folded them, put them in a capsule, and gave them to Lindsey with the following prescription: "Take one a day for a month."

From time to time another couple give each other coupons, like a coupon for a picnic for two, a five-mile hike, or a couple of hours perusing a favorite bookstore.

Learn to Laugh

A first cousin to encouragement is laughter. There are times in life when you can choose to either laugh or cry. When possible, we choose to laugh. Laughter dispels tension. It is good for your physical health, and it is definitely good for your relationship.

When we laugh together, we seem to be more affirming. When we're under stress, we benefit from trying to find a way to lighten things up. Many couples have told us about the fun of pet ownership and how pets can relieve tension. The pressures of med school, work, and being newlyweds were taking a toll on Dan and Laura. After a long day at work, Laura walked into their small apartment and found all three of their cats wearing ties! Dan, in an attempt to make Laura laugh, had tied his ties around the necks of their three cats. (It worked.)

We all have difficult situations in our lives. If we can step back, not take ourselves so seriously, and find something to laugh about, as Dan and Laura did, we can keep our relationship on a positive track.

Helps for Developing a Better Sense of Humor

If laughter doesn't come naturally for you, here are some pointers that may help you become more jovial.

Give yourself permission to be less than perfect.

No one is perfect. Neither you nor your partner! When we don't take ourselves so seriously, we can relax, and it is easier to laugh and see the lighter side of life. Laughing helps us relax. So if joking comes naturally in your relationship, consider yourself fortunate. But there is a fine line between jokes and put-downs. A guiding principle is to laugh *with* your partner but only *at* yourself.

Cultivate humor.

We place cartoons and jokes on our refrigerator door and try to look for the humor in each situation, especially in irritating ones. Recently, as we sat in the Minneapolis airport waiting for our third canceled flight to be rescheduled, I looked at Claudia and said, "My, isn't it fun to be in the jet set?" Claudia's response? "This has to be the life of the rich and famous." Once again, humor came to our rescue. Often when our flights are delayed, we go to the gate where a flight has been called and pretend one of us is leaving. We hug and kiss goodbye. When that flight is loaded, we don't get on because it isn't our flight— we simply go to another gate where another flight has been called and say goodbye all over again.

Some other sources of humor are

- The cartoon section in the daily newspaper
- Joke books and other humorous writing
- Funny stories and jokes from conversations with friends and business associates (We write down memory joggers so we won't forget the punch lines.)
- Funny movies like *Meet the Parents, Son-In-Law,* and *Father of the Bride*

Get some funny friends.

If you're both the serious type, find some funny couples to get to know. Years ago one engaged couple who attended our Marriage Alive seminar was just too serious. Both were opera singers, and both were introspective and intense. We encouraged them to develop some friendships with couples who were not so serious. They took our advice. Having fun-loving friends helped them loosen up, laugh more, and enjoy life in a new way. Humor became one way they encouraged each other.

Date Your Mate

We like to say that fun in marriage is serious business, and one way we put more fun into our marriage is to have dates. Actually we have developed a "dating attitude." We turn almost anything into a date, like running errands together and grocery shopping. Each fall we have a "flu shot date." How could we get excited about that? Well, it's something we need to do for our health, so we simply make it a date. Dave holds my hand while I get my shot and then I hold his when it's his turn. We stop at our favorite coffee shop for a cup of coffee on the way home. Those things you just have to do, you can do them together and call it a date!

What if you're bringing children into the marriage and you have no one to keep the kids? Then put them to bed early and have a stay-at-home date. Candlelight and soft music are very conducive to loving conversations. It just takes a little creativity. Dating is more about being creative than it is about money. As you date each other we encourage you to focus on the positive and take time to laugh together. Your friendship will soar!

Turn to Date Six in your Dating Guide and get ready to encourage each other to leave and cleave!

Date Seven

Celebrating Intimacy, Love, and Romance

So they are no longer two, but one.
Matthew 19:6

Think back to the beginning of your relationship. Do you remember those magical moments when you first began to discover your love for each other? The tingle the first time you held hands? Your first kiss? The intense desire to be with each other?

We do. As we previously shared, Dave was in college at Georgia Tech in Atlanta, and Claudia was at the University of Georgia in Athens early in our relationship. Our thoughts were consumed with each other and with scheming how we could get together on the weekends. Romance was alive and well. For us, all we needed was to just be together. We looked forward to marriage and to a lifetime of celebrating our love.

When we got married, things changed. We didn't have to scheme to get together so romance was no longer "just being together." We, like many couples, entered marriage with different backgrounds, attitudes, and baggage to unpack and process. All these factors complicated our love life. The intense desire for romance and to be together before marriage was replaced by a more complicated set of needs and desires. Keeping intimacy and romance alive was not an easy task.

Allison and Randy are considering marriage but are also concerned about what will happen to romance once they are married. They have several married friends who have turned into boring couch potatoes and never seem to be affectionate when they are around them. Allison and Randy fear that marriage will be the death of romance as they know it.

If you are engaged or seriously considering marriage, perhaps you identify with Allison and Randy. On this date we want to share with you some principles that will help you keep intimacy, love, and romance alive through the years. You will also have the opportunity to talk about how to keep your differing desires and expectations in sync and how to make time for loving each other.

BECOMING ONE

On the last date we looked at Genesis 2:24 and how we are to leave and cleave to one another. When we are following these two principles, we are making our relationship a priority and focusing on using helpful skills to communicate and work through conflict. We are appreciating our differences and looking for ways to encourage each other. A healthy growing relationship is a great foundation for building a creative love life. Let's look at the third part of this verse and discover how in the beginning God created the sexual relationship in marriage both for procreation and for pleasure.

Not only are we to leave and cleave, but in Genesis 2:24 we read we are to become one flesh. It's easy to understand that we need to work at leaving and cleaving, but most don't consider sex in marriage as something you have to work at. Many engaged and newlywed couples we've talked to are convinced that a great sexual relationship happens naturally. And maybe it does while the passion is high. But when life settles down—and it will—the passion may also fade. But it doesn't have to if you take the principle of becoming one seriously.

It is with God's blessing we pursue becoming passionate, sensual lovers, and it's not just for the first few years of marriage. We are to celebrate intimacy, love, and romance through all the years of our marriage. The Scriptures encourage not only sexuality—the physical side of love—but also sensuality—the pleasures like hugs, touches, and other sensations, which encompass the emotional side of love and which are not always associated with making love. The Song of Solomon contains some of the most passionate descriptions of love, romance, and intimacy ever penned. Consider the following excerpts:

- *"Your eyes are doves" (1:15)*
- *"Your lips are like a scarlet ribbon" (4:3)*

- *"Your two breasts are like two fawns, like twin fawns of a gazelle"* *(4:5)*
- *"Your lips drop sweetness as the honeycomb, my bride; milk and honey are under your tongue"* *(4:11)*
- *"His body is like polished ivory decorated with sapphires"* *(5:14)*
- *"His mouth is sweetness itself"* *(5:16)*

In *A Lasting Promise*, the authors challenge couples to develop both the sexual and sensual sides of love when they write, "Couples who enjoy the most rewarding physical unions realize that, in a sense, all of marriage is foreplay. The foundations of emotional, intellectual, and spiritual closeness, along with nonsexual sensuality, provide the basis for great experiences of love in sexual union."[1] So how can you make sure you keep both the sexual and sensual sides of love alive in your marriage? We suggest starting by affirming that a healthy love life blends both the emotional and physical sides of love and is like a shining star with many facets.

FACETS OF A STAR-STUDDED LOVE LIFE[2]

In a national survey we asked couples what they considered to be the best aspects of their love life. While the responses varied, several themes emerged as essential components for a truly healthy love life: trust, mutuality, honesty, intimacy, affection, and sex. On this date you will have the opportunity to look closer at each facet. It is our hope that this will help you build a star-studded love life.

Trust—Feeling Safe with Each Other

Trust is a basic component of any friendship and is essential in a romantic relationship. Trust develops when you feel safe with your partner. It also develops when you know you can share yourself with your partner and your partner will not harm or betray you.

Realistically, in a relationship that is as close as marriage is, from time to time we let each other down. When trust is broken, it needs to be rebuilt before it is possible to work on the other aspects of a love relationship. Easily taken for granted when present and devastating when absent, the bond of trust is fundamental to intimacy. Let us encourage you to seek constantly to build and affirm the trust that exists between you. Here are some simple trust builders:

- Helping out when your partner is on overload
- Saying you're going to do it—like calling when you're going to be late—and actually do it
- Giving an honest compliment
- Apologizing when you are wrong
- Accepting your partner's apology without saying "I told you so!"
- Keeping your sense of humor when things go wrong

Mutuality—Freely Choosing to Love Each Other

Each partner must want to be in the relationship. Having a mutual relationship involves a decision to choose each other above all others and to make your relationship a priority—to be willing to grow together and to adapt to each other's changing needs over the years.

We realize that there will be some times when you would like to take a hike or just have some time alone, but in a mutual relationship, partners generally like to be together—even with the normal ups and downs all relationships experience.

We all know what it feels like when someone we are with doesn't want to be with us. Perhaps you can think of a sour blind date or when your partner convinced you to go to a movie you knew you would hate. I still remember the time Claudia insisted that I go with her to a lecture on how to have a successful marriage. The presenter left me cold. I didn't want to be there. I felt that Claudia manipulated and coerced me into going, and I would have rather been anywhere else. Obviously, I got nothing out of the lecture!

If Claudia had been less insistent, we might have found an activity that would have pleased us both. For example, going out for a mutually agreeable dinner would have fostered mutuality. Forcing me to the lecture certainly didn't!

Power plays and manipulation destroy the potential for intimacy, love, and romance. When one partner always wants his own way and resorts to nagging, threatening, or manipulating to get it, the relationship is sabotaged.

Think about how good it feels when your partner makes you feel loved and desired through a twinkle in the eye, a gentle caress of the hand, or a loving comment. This quiet understanding naturally breeds security, confidence, and romance, and you will naturally be mutually devoted to each other. Following are some ways to demonstrate your devotion to your partner:

- Frame a picture of the two of you.
- Create your own greeting card and express your love.
- Send a special email to say, "I'm thinking about you right now."
- Hug for ten seconds.
- Give your partner a sincere compliment.
- Take a walk together.
- Give your partner a long-stemmed rose.

Honesty—Openly Communicating Your True Feelings

Honesty is as necessary to a healthy love life as sunlight is to flowers and trees. If spouses do not have the ability to relate their needs and desires truthfully and without manipulation, their love life will falter along the way. While applying frankness to conversational topics like intimacy and sex takes vulnerability, commitment, and practice, the rewards of being open and honest are well worth it. King Solomon in Proverbs 24:26 summed it up well: "An honest answer is like a kiss on the lips." Remember the helpful communication skills you practiced on Dates Three and Four? Here's a quick review of some helpful tips for soliciting honest answers from each other:

- Start sentences with "I."
- Avoid "you" statements and "why" questions.
- Resist saying "never" and "always."
- Give five positive statements for every negative statement.
- Generously use the words "please" and "thank you."
- Develop your own secret love language.

Intimacy—Being Soul Mates and Feeling Close

Based on trust, freely entered into by both partners, and fueled by honesty, intimacy is the intangible quality of unity, understanding, and synergy that can move a relationship to the deep level as soul mates and lovers. In *Saving Your Second Marriage Before It Starts*, Les and Leslie Parrott write, "Intimacy fills our heart's deepest longings for closeness and acceptance.... The fulfillment of love hinges on closeness, sharing, communication, honesty, and support. As one heart given in exchange for another, marriage provides the deepest and most radical expressions of intimacy."[3]

Like all the previously mentioned components of a healthy love life, intimacy ebbs and flows over the life of a marriage. Other factors affect intimacy. Children can challenge marital intimacy. If you're considering marrying someone with children or you have children from a previous marriage, you will need to work extra hard to keep intimacy on the front burner. When intimacy is low in a relationship, partners are not motivated to communicate on anything more than a superficial level, physical contact is perfunctory if not completely missing, and marital satisfaction and joy are lacking.

On the other hand, couples who experience a high level of intimacy often laugh a little more and a little louder, are more affectionate, and are more likely to feel understood, accepted, and loved. Developing intimacy in your relationship will help to encourage the sharing of dreams, needs, fears, and desires. It takes intentionality and time, but working at staying intimate with your partner is an investment you will want to make. Consider the following intimacy developers:

- Write a love letter.
- Make a list of why you are soul mates.
- Share three things about each other that you really like.
- Listen with your heart.
- Protect your private times together.
- Pray together.

Affection—Giving Joy and Comfort to Each Other

Affection is an important part of a creative love life. However, many times the tedium of everyday life creeps in and fills the space that should be saved for laughter, fun, and pleasure. Lack of time to nurture the sensual side of your love life can lead to misunderstandings, and those can lead to less desire to take time to talk and resolve issues. When a relationship loses its spark and joy, it loses much of its purpose and grounding. Too often this leaves partners wondering why they are in the relationship in the first place.

Throughout the years of a marriage, spouses need to recapture being affectionate with each other. Giving affection and having fun together should be the most natural thing in the world, but unfortunately it isn't. That's why you have to work on it. Consider the following ways to express affection:

- Share a cup of coffee while listening to your favorite CD.
- Laugh together as you share a joke.
- Give a one-minute shoulder rub.
- Give a spontaneous hug and a kiss.
- Light a candle together.
- Eat a banana split with two spoons.
- Cuddle on the couch.
- Whisper "sweet nothings" in each other's ears.

Sex—Joining Together Physically and Loving Each Other

The culmination of a great love life is sex. Remember, God created sexuality, and it is his plan that you experience a great love life throughout the seasons of your marriage. A pleasurable sexual experience is the most intense and intimate thing a couple can share. In their book *The Good Marriage*, Judith Wallerstein and Sandra Blakeslee emphasize the importance of sex. "It is very important for all couples to find ways to protect their privacy, to cherish their sexual relationship, to guard it fiercely. A richly rewarding and stable sex life is not just a fringe benefit; it is the central task of marriage. In a good marriage, sex and love are inseparable. Sex serves a very serious function in maintaining both the quality and stability of the relationship, replenishing emotional reserves, and strengthening the marital bond."[4]

Consider the following marriage love builders:

- Plan time in your schedule for love making. Schedule appointments.
- Eat right, exercise, and get enough sleep.
- Learn how to give a massage.
- Read a book together on sex.
- Be adventuresome; be a learner.
- Learn to please each other.
- Do the unexpected.

Understanding the facets of love—trust, mutuality, honesty, intimacy, affection, and sex—will help you create your own great love life.

Far from being a marital add-on, a healthy, creative love life is a key to a good marriage, but to achieve it you need to understand each other's expectations.

UNDERSTANDING EXPECTATIONS

If you want to celebrate intimacy, love, and romance in your marriage, you will need to try to understand each other's expectations. Rare is the couple who want the same things from their love life or who like the same types of pleasure in the same quantities. More typical are two people with very different likes and expectations trying their best to sort out a satisfying middle ground. Partners need to know what enhances or builds intimacy for each of them. For women, emotional intimacy usually precedes sexual intimacy, and for men, sexual intimacy creates emotional intimacy. So how can you identify and verbalize your expectations? Basically, you need to know two things: what you want and what your partner wants.

It's not that easy. We carry so much baggage with us that sorting out what is truly important to us in a love life can be a confusing process. Perhaps you have a media-created image of what intimacy, love, and romance should be. Movies often portray unrealistic images and make our expectations unrealistic. In addition, sometimes it is difficult to understand or verbalize your own needs and desires.

Talking about your expectations is one of the most intimate times you will ever share with your partner and should be initiated in an atmosphere of trust, unconditional love, and acceptance. We realize there will be differences in your desires and in how adventurous you are. One caution: If one partner is having difficulty expressing expectations, be patient, gentle, and accepting.

For us, without a doubt, the most frustrating situations have been when we misunderstood each other's expectations. This usually happens when we don't talk about them. So we have three tips to help you begin to talk about your expectations: (1) be verbal, (2) be specific, and (3) be realistic.

Be Verbal

One of the greatest things you can do to create understanding is to talk about your expectations. This will help you get on the same page, but don't be surprised if your expectations are quite different. Talking about them can be a great starting point for better understanding each other's needs and desires.

Let us also encourage you to talk about what is sensual for you and what you can do to promote and protect the sensual side of love. The authors of *Fighting for Your Marriage* write how sensual talking is an art and how it is one of the best ways to enhance your love relationship, although rarely used. They give examples of sharing with your partner how attracted you are to her, how sexy she is, how much you love and care for him, how much you enjoy his touch, or the pleasure of a lingering kiss during which time seems to stop.[5]

Be Specific

When talking about what you want out of your love relationship, be specific. In some ways, talking about the specifics of your love life is like learning a new language. It may seem awkward at first, but you need to develop your sex vocabulary. How will you know what the other likes unless you talk about it? Too often we just assume that the other should automatically know what we want or need.

We also encourage you to talk about any fears and inhibitions you might have. One of you may be much more inhibited than the other, so a major part of talking it out may be the willingness to listen or to be vulnerable to the other. You may want to discuss other specific issues that you will face—such as how much time will you allocate to building a creative love life (more about that later).

Be Realistic

Each season of marriage offers challenges and opportunities for growth, and in each season you will want to reexamine your expectations. What is realistic at one time in your marriage may be totally unrealistic at another time. Start by considering where you are right now. Is this a first marriage for both? Or is this a second marriage for one or both of you? Today almost half of all marriages are second marriages, and a significant number marry with kids. If you are bringing children into the marriage, it is important to consider how they will affect your love life and what expectations are realistic. Whatever your circumstances, your love life can be the icing on your marriage cake if you take the time to discover how to love each other.

Just Married

Regardless of how well you know each other before marriage, after marriage you will make new discoveries! Consider the following three suggestions for newlyweds.

1. Become learners.

We learn to respond sexually, as we learn anything else, by working at it. We don't assume built-in knowledge in our professions, parenting children, or hanging wallpaper—neither should we assume that being married makes us great lovers. Achieving success in any endeavor requires work, and sex is no exception. Even when things are hectic and crazy, you need to look for time to invest in your sexual relationship.

Consider organizing your own sex study program. You might want to read through the Song of Solomon together. Or you may want to choose helpful books to read together (see Helpful Resources, page 141).

Years ago when we were newlyweds, few "how-to" books were available, but we managed to find a few. Slowly, we began to learn what worked best for us. The guiding principle was that we wanted to please each other and that it was pleasurable for both.

2. Become explorers.

Talking and reading about sex isn't enough. Be willing to become explorers and discover what you like and don't like. Doesn't that sound simple? Yes, but it's not that easy. For some, fear that they can't perform or won't be exciting to their mate causes them to hold back and to be more inhibited. One thing that helped us when we were adjusting to marriage was to plan times of sensual non-demand touching to discover how to pleasure each other. The goal for these times was not sex—as a matter of fact, for this exercise sexual intercourse was off-limits. This helped us relax, feel comfortable with each other, and eliminated the pressure of performance.

3. Become other-centered.

It is easy to become "me-centered" and lose your sensitivity to your partner. Sometimes it's easy to forget that the best way to really please yourself is to please your partner. When you focus on pleasing the other, you may find that you will be less self-conscious and will overcome any lingering inhibitions. Study your partner and learn what pleases him or her. You may find one of you tends to be visual while the other tends to respond to tenderness and talk.

Learn all you can during the discovery years because little ones may be just up ahead, and babies bring with them many challenges to surmount if you want to hang on to intimacy, love, and romance!

Just Married with Children

If you are entering marriage with children, this section is especially for you! Recently on *Good Morning America*, a couple was interviewed who had three sets of twins—all under six years of age! The wife had brought one set of twins into the marriage from a previous marriage. Soon after they married, they had twins and while the twins were still babies, they got pregnant with another set of twins. For them, realistic expectations at this stage of family life may simply be maintenance and survival.

You may not have twins, but if you have young kids, you will face extra challenges in fostering intimacy and romance. Before you know it, everything else may seem to come first—the baby, your career advancement, your friends, your social life. Your love life can become an obligation or something you just don't think about. Romance—what's that? At this stage of marriage, it is vital that you talk about your expectations and devise a workable plan—even if you are totally exhausted!

For us, the hardest time in our love life was when we had three children under the age of five. Our expectations were different, and the way we handled exhaustion was different. When Claudia was exhausted, she needed sleep to recharge. Dave could be as exhausted as Claudia but seemed to always have a spare "ever-ready battery" when it came to our love life.

When all the children went to school at the same time, it was a great day for us. We looked forward to having relief from twenty-four hour parenting, and we anticipated more flexibility in our schedule and more opportunities to revitalize our love life, which was stuck in a survival mode. With some creative scheduling, we managed to carve out time each week to meet at home without the kids around. It was a love life saver for us.

If you are marrying with older children, you will need to keep talking about your wants, desires, and expectations. Recently we met a couple who had just gotten engaged on the top of the Eiffel Tower. So romantic! But when they told us they were each bringing three teenagers into their marriage, we told them to hang on to all the romance they could find!

Few times are more stressful than when you have teenagers in the house. There's always a crisis, and they tend to stay up later than you do. Don't let them zap all your emotional energy! We claimed Saturday mornings as "our time" because our teenagers happily slept until noon! During our time on Saturdays we refused to talk about our teenagers. Instead we focused on us. Whatever you do, keep your sense of humor. This too shall pass.

MAKE TIME FOR LOVING

In whatever season of life you are entering marriage, you will need to focus on making time for loving each other. Marital experts are now predicting that the major problem couples will be facing in future years is decreasing interest in sex![6] God forbid! This is not his plan, nor should it be yours. But unless you intentionally make time for your love life, you may end up one of the statistics. Please note that we are not saying "find time for your love life." Instead we are saying "make time!" There is a difference.

We all have to deal with the love life zapper that some call the "hurry sickness"—just too much to do and too little time to do it. All couples are susceptible, especially parents of young children. The University of Creighton study on newlyweds says that those with children have the most distressed marriages of those who stay together. They note that some of this is around having little time or energy for an intimate relationship.[7]

But those without children also have to fight for time for their love life. Whatever your circumstances, let us caution you, don't get so busy that you neglect being sensual and sexual with each other. Give priority to your couple relationship! If you are realistic in what you expect, and if you make time for each other, you can be lifelong lovers. Remember to polish each facet of your love life. You can experience true intimacy, love, and romance.

Romance Enhancers

- Celebrate something like your first date.
- Fly a kite.
- Go fishing.
- Read a funny book.
- Visit an old haunt.
- Reverse roles for a day.
- Pick wild flowers.
- Go on a picnic.
- Go window shopping.
- Buy matching coffee cups.
- Watch the sun set.
- Ride bikes.
- Roast marshmallows in the fireplace.
- Make a tape of the reasons you love your spouse. Wrap it in a silk scarf or tie.
- Go to a play.
- Start a hobby.
- Buy new cologne or perfume.
- Rent a classic romance video.
- Place red heart stickers everywhere for a week.
- Fill your Christmas stockings in July.
- Surprise your partner with season tickets to a sporting event, symphony, or theater.
- Build a campfire.

Now it's time for another great date!
Turn to Date Seven in the
Dating Guide and have fun talking
about love, intimacy, and romance!

Date Eight

Realizing Roles and Planning for Family

Beloved, let us love so well,
Our work shall still be better for our love,
And still our love be sweeter for our work,
And both commended for the sake of each,
By all true workers and true lovers born.
Elizabeth B. Browning

We asked a group of teenagers what they wanted in a mate when they married. One girl said she wanted to have an exciting career as well as five children, and she was sure that her husband would share home responsibilities fifty-fifty. A boy in the same group said he wanted an "old-fashioned" wife just like his mom, one who would find cleaning the house, cooking, washing, and ironing his clothes creative and exciting. We looked at each other and thought if these two were to get together, they were going to need help!

You may be thinking that this boy's idea is totally out-of-date and needs to transition into the twenty-first century. And sure enough, when we asked seriously dating and engaged couples how they plan to share household responsibilities, the majority answered fifty-fifty. But when we ask newlywed couples how they are sharing household responsibilities, guess who is doing the majority of the chores? If you think the wife is, you're correct. What happens along the way that changes pre-marriage expectations about roles and responsibilities to the reality that one ends up with more than half the work?

One answer is lack of communication and lack of having a plan. Many times, couples don't talk about roles and responsibilities before marriage. They just assume everything will work out—then life happens. They slide into roles without ever talking about them. But the subject of roles and responsibilities is too important to ignore. On Date Eight you will get the opportunity to talk about this critical subject.

David Olson in his book *Empowering Couples* points out that the division of household tasks is strongly related to couple satisfaction. He writes, "Happy couples are much more likely to not feel concerned that one partner is doing more than his or her share of household tasks than unhappy couples.... Happy couples also tend to make decisions jointly and to allocate household chores based on interest and skills rather than traditional roles."[1]

REALIZING YOUR ROLES

If couples who share responsibilities are happier, how can you make sure you will equally share the load? We suggest that you begin by assessing your responsibilities—or those you plan to assume when you are married.

Assess Your Responsibilities

The first step in assessing responsibilities is to consider what you perceive your and your future spouse's responsibilities will be inside as well as outside the home. Do your lists appear to be balanced?

For instance, if one will work outside the home part time and the other will work a sixty-hour week, the part-timer would need to help balance the seesaw by carrying more of the load at home. But for now, let's assume you will both have equal commitments outside the home. The important question becomes, "How will you pull together as a team at home?"

In spite of the many unrealistic stereotypes today, we are delighted to see so many couples pulling together as they wrestle with jobs, children, and busy schedules. But it's not always easy.

Jim, forty, and Jean, thirty-eight, are engaged to be married. Both were widowed. In each of their previous marriages their roles were more traditional than Jean wants them to be in their upcoming marriage. Previously their roles worked well when their children were young. Jean was a stay-at-home mom, but now circumstances have changed.

After Jean's husband died, she started her own interior design business. Initially she worked part time out of her home and actually met Jim when he hired her to redesign his office. Now her business has grown to the point that she works full time and a number of her appointments are in the evenings.

Here's the dilemma. When they marry, they will bring together both sets of children (ages eleven, thirteen, fourteen, and sixteen) and will both work full time outside the home. Jim's first wife took care of all the home details as well as major parenting responsibilities. Since his wife's death, Jim has been both mom and dad to his two teenage sons, and he is looking forward to the possibility that Jean will cut back on her work and take up some of the slack at home. So how will marriage change their roles?

From Jim's perspective, his daily routine will not change drastically—except he will have some help at home and with his sons. Jean's daily schedule will be another story. Jean has no desire to cut back— she loves her job and gets a lot of fulfillment from being creative. While she is used to juggling work and parenting her two daughters, suddenly having two teenage boys around is going to add to the stress and to her workload at home. Already, before the wedding, tension is mounting.

To help plan realistically for their future roles, they each listed potential home responsibilities that both might be expected to assume. When Jean saw Jim's list, she knew they had some work to do to balance their roles and responsibilities. Here's what Jim wrote as he thought about what his responsibilities would be and what he thought Jean's responsibilities might be. His two lists looked like this:

Jim's Responsibilities at Home
1. Take care of the yard
2. Keep cars maintained
3. Keep family financial records
4. Coach sons' soccer team

Jean's Responsibilities at Home
1. Prepare meals
2. Grocery shop
3. Do laundry for family of six
4. Keep the house clean
5. Keep track of children's activities
6. Help children with homework

It is obvious that Jim and Jean need to talk and compromise before they say "I do." Jim's list of home responsibilities are important and will take time, but he could accomplish them on the weekends. The areas of responsibility Jim listed for Jean are not as flexible and will daily demand more than she will be able to give after working all day. They need to talk more realistically about how to distribute the load at home.

Define Your Roles

Whether this is a first or second marriage, you may find it very helpful to talk about your roles before you say "I do." The following list may help you begin thinking about this topic:

_____ Shopping	_____ Vacuuming
_____ Preparing for meals	_____ Taking out garbage
_____ Making beds	_____ Cleaning out closets
_____ Caring for the lawn	_____ Paying the bills
_____ Maintaining cars	_____ Balancing the checkbook
_____ Cleaning bathrooms	_____ Preparing tax returns
_____ Doing laundry	_____ Doing household repairs
_____ Ironing	_____ Scheduling appointments
_____ Dusting	_____ Keeping financial records
_____ Buying groceries	_____ Returning DVDs and videos
_____ Caring for pets	_____ Other _____

You may want to add to our list other household jobs and responsibilities. Then you can look at the list and talk about who naturally enjoys doing the various jobs. Also, it will be helpful to discuss those jobs you enjoy doing the least. Then you can go through the list again from the grid of who can do the job better.

When we did this exercise, we discovered that Claudia doesn't mind doing the laundry, so she took that on. Dave likes to grill, so he took over that responsibility. He also enjoys keeping track of our finances—a job that gives Claudia headaches! While talking through our list, Claudia immediately conceded that Dave was the best bathroom cleaner in ten states!

The brutal reality is that no one will choose or want to do some jobs. Compromise and understanding are important parts of the process. We have found that we can handle stress better if just one other person understands how we feel. You can be that other person for your spouse.

Once Jim and Jean evaluated their lists, Jim became aware that when they married, he would need to participate more in sharing the workload at home. Who does what is not as important as the philosophy of sharing the load together.

Jim and Jean actually came up with a reasonable and realistic plan. They decided that they would recruit their children for jobs around the house. Jean's friends gave her a household shower. Gifts included a Crock-Pot and a couple of cookbooks for easy one-dish meals. With the Crock-Pot and a little planning, she (or even Jim) might be able to have dinner on the way before leaving for work. They also talked about initially hiring a personal chef for the first couple of months. Jim agreed to be the homework monitor and to help with special school assignments.

For heavy jobs around the house, Jim and Jean agreed to hire a cleaning service once a month. Once married, Jim and Jean will certainly have other adjustments to make, but talking about roles before marriage is a great start in fostering better understanding.

Talk, Talk, and Listen!

It's one thing to talk about roles before you say "I do," and another thing to actually do what you say you're going to do after the wedding. Curt doesn't remember talking about this subject when we were dating. I (Natelle) am sure that we did; however, I don't think Curt was listening! As I remember it, we talked about how we would both pursue careers and share household responsibilities fifty-fifty. I thought that Curt was agreeable to doing things differently from the model he had grown up in. Wrong!

He was more than happy to let me (the pleaser, conflict-avoider) do more than my share. In fact, I did all the grocery shopping, cooking, dusting, vacuuming, scrubbing, laundry, ironing, gift buying, and letter writing. Curt's job was to put gas in our only car and to get the oil changed (he didn't even do it himself!). Curt supported my having a job as long as I could get everything else done. It didn't take long before I began to feel taken for granted. My resentment and Curt's apathy were not a recipe for closeness. So, take it from someone who has been there, done that, and knows there is a better way. Discuss roles and responsibilities and then be prepared to negotiate, negotiate, and negotiate!

Do you think our experience is totally outdated and that you don't need to be concerned with role issues? You might want to pause and think about how roles become established in a marriage. Many times couples drift into roles based on what was modeled in their family of origin. Do you come from similar or different backgrounds as to roles in marriage? Do you agree with the roles your parents modeled? On Date Eight you will have the opportunity to talk about how you want to blend your roles together. Keep in mind that compromise is crucial for building a healthy relationship.

PLANNING FOR FAMILY

Another major topic for Date Eight is talking about your future hopes and dreams concerning children. What are your expectations concerning family planning? While having a baby is exciting, we need to alert you that marriage satisfaction dips big time for most couples when they become parents. Because of the time pressures children bring, couples need to be reminded to keep fun and friendship in their marriage. And not all couples agree on if and when to have children.

Bill and Susan

Bill and Susan talked about almost everything before they married, but the subject of children never came up. Susan got the shock of her life when one day she told Bill, "I'm really ready to have a baby. I don't want to wait any longer. Let's get pregnant."

"Get pregnant?" Bill said in unbelief. "I don't want to be a father! Children could destroy a marriage. Besides, we're older. I never knew you wanted to have a baby at your age!"

Susan responded, "What do you mean at my age? I'm only thirty-eight. Sure, my biological clock *is* ticking. That's why I really want to have a baby right now."

"Listen, Susan, I want to make myself perfectly clear—no children, no baby, not now, not ever!"

Unfortunately, Bill and Susan's story does not have a happy ending. Susan became more obsessed with wanting to get pregnant. Bill became more obstinate about never wanting children. While they saw eye-to-eye on most issues, they just couldn't resolve their differences regarding this core family value. The next year they divorced. Perhaps if they had communicated and talked about family planning before they married, they might have spared each other considerable heartache.

Neil and Debbie

Even couples who both agree they want to have children may be hesitant to make the commitment. Neil and Debbie have been married for three years, and Debbie's biological clock is also ticking. Still she has reservations, "I would love to have a baby, but I don't want to hurt our marriage. Isn't it just downhill after you have kids?"

"No," we told her. "If you keep your marriage a priority, children can actually enrich your marriage!"

If you are among the majority of couples who will choose parenthood, we have encouragement for you as well as some caution. While children will change your life and bring new demands and stress, your dual roles as partner and parent can actually complement one another.

When Baby Makes Three

What has the energy of an atomic bomb, provides more entertainment than a Broadway show, and weighs about seven and a half pounds? It's the arrival of that first baby! The first child brings big changes for his or her parents. Nothing will ever be the same again.

We hear much about the strain parenting places on the marriage relationship. Words like *tired, exhausted,* and *burned out* take on new meaning. But we hear little about how having children can enrich a marriage. Consider the following ways your marriage may benefit from your role as parents.

Children Will Remind You That You're One

Little ones running around are a continual reminder that in a real, tangible way you and your spouse are "one." Each time you see Junior's toes you have to admit they are just like Dad's, or Susie's big smile is a picture of Mom's smile that won you over.

Children Will Foster Teamwork

Parenting definitely calls for a team approach. It is difficult for one parent to do it all. Brainstorm ways to lessen stressful situations, like "morning madness." One can assume the responsibility for breakfast while the other makes sure the kids get up, get dressed, and stay on schedule. At night when the kids are in bed, together you can talk about how to handle extra stresses you may be experiencing. Just knowing one other person understands your stress helps tremendously in handling it appropriately.

Children Will Promote Appreciation

Because the responsibilities of parenting leave less free time for two, you'll learn to appreciate each other in a new way. To be alone together is a real treat and one worth working for.

Children Will Promote Creativity

If you spend time together when your children are small, it will stretch your creativity. Consider the following:

- Plan a "Progressive Errand Date." Group your errands together. You can have time alone in the car as you visit the cleaners, post office, drugstore, and, on your way home, the frozen yogurt stand.
- Go to a park that has a tennis court. Give your children plenty of balls, and the two of you can sit down and talk. The tennis court becomes a gigantic playpen!
- Grab that time when your kids are at soccer practice. If you need to be close by, walk around the field together and talk.
- Plan a getaway the same weekend as the band trip.

Children Will Check Your Communication and Keep You Honest

It's amazing what you say or don't say when little ears are listening. You're the model. It's enough to make us all stop and think before we speak. Just doing that would benefit any marriage.

Children Will Give Great Rewards

It is rewarding to see your children launched into life. And part of that reward is all the memories of how your children enriched your life and marriage. You'll never run out of things to reminisce about. But you will also send them off into life with numerous ways your marriage has enriched their lives!

If you have children you will have the opportunity in your upcoming marriage to pass on traditions and values to the next generation. What family traditions are most precious to you? How can you model your core beliefs to your children? In the next chapter, "Developing Spiritual Intimacy," you will have the opportunity to talk about the deeper issues in life.

But now it's time to turn to Date Eight in the Dating Guide and have fun talking about your future roles and potential family!

Date Nine

Developing Spiritual Intimacy

God the best maker of all marriages,
Combine your hearts as one.
Shakespeare

For the last eight dates we have focused on helping you build your relationship as you look forward to marriage. Now let's consider the role you want spirituality to play in your lives together and how building spiritual intimacy with God and with one another will enrich your future marriage.

You might begin by considering when and where you feel close to God. Is it when you are worshiping together at church with other believers? Do you experience spiritual closeness when you pray and meditate, or when you study the Bible together? Perhaps it is when you sing praise songs or hymns or play a praise CD and simply listen to the words. Others feel really close to God when they are out in nature.

We feel a special closeness to God when we are walking on a beach or climbing a mountain path. Seeing the majesty of God's creation causes our hearts to resonate with one another and to want to worship our Creator. Over the years, we have also experienced deep spiritual intimacy in the hard places of life—the loss of a loved one or a stressful time such as an illness, financial challenge, or relationship struggle.

While many different circumstances can draw us to God, spiritual intimacy is not a mystic, passive experience. Spiritual intimacy can be cultivated. A starting place is to consider the things you enjoy doing together that foster intimacy with God. Also, consider the spiritual beliefs you are bringing into your marriage. Did you grow up in a Christian home, or are you just beginning your spiritual journey? If you and your future spouse are from different spiritual backgrounds, how do you plan to handle that after marriage?

In a survey of over 21,000 couples, 89 percent of happy couples are satisfied with how they express their spiritual values and beliefs.[1] To us it just makes sense to discuss your own spiritual values and beliefs with each other before your marriage. It is another way you can get to know each other better. Also, you may find that if you talk about spiritual values before you say "I do," it will be easier when children come along.

Actually, numerous other studies suggest that having a shared spiritual dimension in your life has a favorable impact on marriage. For instance, couples who frequently pray together are twice as likely as those who pray less often to describe their marriages as being highly romantic.[2] Also, those who are religious are less likely to divorce, have higher levels of satisfaction, and higher levels of commitment.[3]

Some even go so far to say that developing a shared belief system is central to having a healthy sexual relationship.[4] These findings make sense to us because having a shared faith binds you together in the midst of daily living and dealing with problems.

Certainly marriage offers a unique opportunity for intimacy. It provides the time and opportunity for growing together spiritually. So on this date, focus on how to develop spiritual intimacy through developing a shared core belief system. Then look at how these core values will impact your upcoming marriage.

We realize not everyone is at the same place on their spiritual journey. However, we believe that all have some core belief system, and your core beliefs shape who you are and how you relate to others. It is a wonderful starting place to talk about spirituality.

What are your shared core beliefs? What do you believe about God, life, death, family, marriage, and so on? Perhaps you have never really talked together about your core beliefs. If you are willing to ask yourself hard questions and seek until you find answers, you can certainly benefit from this date. We believe that those who pursue this topic can develop spiritual intimacy as well as couple intimacy. In the following pages we (the Arps) will share our personal spiritual pilgrimage in hopes that our experience might encourage you on your own spiritual journey.

OUR SEARCH FOR SPIRITUAL INTIMACY

Our own spiritual search began with a rather traumatic event after we were married. Four years into our marriage, we were delighted that we were going to become parents. In the last weeks of the pregnancy, we discovered that our baby was in a breech position. The doctors assured us that all was fine—until the actual birth.

"God, please let this baby live!" I prayed while lying on the sterile table in the delivery room at Madigan General Military Hospital. We had spent the last three weeks moving into our Army quarters at Fort Lewis, Washington, and getting the nursery ready for the birth of our first child.

Moving back to the United States from serving with the Army in Europe in the final weeks of my pregnancy was risky. But we had no other choice. I remember that day, which is etched forever in my memory.

At the moment I delivered our first child, I didn't hear him cry, welcoming in the first breaths of life. I didn't hear the joyous cheers and congratulations of the attending physicians and nurses. Instead I heard medical professionals anxiously consulting each other as they hovered over our child. When I could finally hear what they were saying, I realized that my baby wasn't breathing. Those tortured first few minutes seemed like hours. I knew by the faces of the doctors and nurses that what was going on was not normal and not something that could be fixed by a quick bottom slap. My newborn baby was in trouble.

At the moment I realized our firstborn son was fighting for his life, I instinctively turned to God for supernatural intervention on our child's behalf. And moments later, David Jarrett Arp sucked in glorious, life-giving air, claiming this world as his own and us as his parents. My prayer had been answered!

Though some might write this experience off as coincidence, we do not. I was serious when I turned to God for help. And so strongly feeling his presence when my simple prayer was answered, we both knew this was the beginning of our spiritual quest.

Our Spiritual Discovery

Before Jarrett's birth, we had never paid much attention to our spiritual lives or our core beliefs. Until that fateful day, our lives had run pretty smoothly, and we didn't feel the need to examine them too deeply.

Relating to each other was easy for us. We were secure in our love. Sure, we had the occasional disagreement, but we didn't experience any serious stress until our first son was born. Now we had just survived the trauma of an intercontinental move, a difficult birth with a life-challenging spiritual experience, and the incredibly common stresses of a colicky baby. Even though we were committed to each other and to spending some time making good on Claudia's delivery room commitment to find and understand God, we were suffering under the weight of life. Our marriage began to suffer.

For the first time we began to snap at each other and argue. It seemed that the harder we tried to make our marriage work, the worse things got. We weren't getting off to a good start as partners in parenting, and we didn't have the resources or skills to find any spiritual answers.

Fast-forward a couple of years. We were out of the Army and had moved to Atlanta, Georgia, and were now expecting our second child. During this time we renewed friendships with friends from our college days and joined in a local fellowship. We were raised in the Christian tradition and, finally, the spiritual seed planted in our childhood took root. We understood spiritual truths that in the past had eluded us. And as we watched our energetic two-year-old, it wasn't difficult for us to believe there was a God who hears and answers prayers.

During this time it helped that we were actively seeking spiritual answers. We read the Bible and found in the Gospels someone whose love for us was greater than anything we had ever experienced. We encountered Jesus Christ. Our path to spiritual understanding was illuminated by God's love that to this day we find utterly amazing. And as God began to be more real to us, we experienced true spiritual intimacy in our marriage. It was as if we had been plugged into a new power source. Finding forgiveness, security, and significance in our relationship with Jesus Christ freed us to love and accept each other in a deeper way.

Our newfound faith gave us the courage to take risks and to be willing to grow. Now, many years later, our spiritual journey continues. We still have a close, personal relationship with Christ, and our faith in God has impacted our lives in so many ways. Chief among them is our marriage relationship.

WHAT IS SPIRITUAL INTIMACY?

To us personally, spiritual intimacy means emotional closeness with God through our relationship with Jesus Christ, and this contributes to emotional closeness with each other. The authors of *A Lasting Promise* write that "spiritual intimacy goes to the deepest and most vulnerable parts of your soul. To go there together, you need the kind of trust, safety, and security that are born of commitment and respectful handling of issues and problems in your relationship."[5]

Les and Leslie Parrott shed light on the value of spiritual intimacy when they write about a shared commitment to spiritual discovery in their book *Saving Your Marriage Before It Starts.* "The spiritual dimension of marriage is a practical source of food for marital growth and health. No single factor does more to cultivate oneness and a meaningful sense of purpose in marriage than a shared commitment to spiritual discovery. It is the ultimate hunger of our souls."[6] We know that in our own spiritual journey, our commitment to spiritual intimacy has helped to satisfy our hungry souls!

Discovering Your Core Beliefs

Where are you on your journey? Are you and your partner at similar places? We know that opposites attract and that partners do not have to agree on everything, but some fundamentals must govern the relationship. Your shared core beliefs are the building blocks of an intimate relationship. On this date you will have the opportunity to talk about what you believe and about the fundamental values that you share.

We discovered that our common faith and beliefs gave us the opportunity to develop a deeper personal intimacy with each other. Years ago we chose Ecclesiastes 4:9–12 as a theme for our marriage. To us, it describes the kind of spiritual intimacy we want for our marriage.

> *Two are better than one, because they have a good return for their work: If one falls down, his friend can help him up. But pity the man who falls and has no one to help him up! Also, if two lie down together, they will keep warm. But how can one keep warm alone? Though one may be overpowered, two can defend themselves. A cord of three strands is not quickly broken.*

In our marriage, we like to think about Dave being one strand, Claudia being one strand, and God's Holy Spirit being the third strand that holds it all together when our individual strands are frayed. We see our marriage as a partnership with each other and with God. Many times we let each other down, and it's then that we look to our third strand to keep our cord strong—to hold us together when our individual strands are frayed.

A story from the Arp archives illustrates what we are talking about. Years ago we had the opportunity to move again to Germany. We were only given six weeks' notice, and we disagreed about the move. It was a crisis point. At the time we had three small children and were happily settled in Knoxville, Tennessee. Who would consider moving? Dave did. I didn't.

We spent many long hours discussing the pros and cons of such a drastic move. Dave saw the opportunities, adventure, and challenge of a new job. I saw giving up my family, friends, and a home that I loved and facing all the complications of moving and surviving in a foreign culture with three small, active boys. Dave was challenged. I was scared. Time was running out.

We prayed together, and we prayed separately about the possible move. Dave got peace. I got panic! Finally, the deadline drew near. Were we about to give up the opportunity of a lifetime? There were no easy answers or solutions. We just couldn't agree!

Without the basis of our lifelong commitment to each other, our shared purpose in life, and our relationship with Christ, I don't know what would have happened. I'll never forget the feeling of being totally out of sync with Dave. He felt so strongly about not passing up this opportunity. Finally I realized he felt stronger about us going than I felt about us staying. I also realized that his feelings were based on how our gifts meshed with the job opportunity, coupled with a strong conviction that God was actually calling us to Europe.

My opinion was based on fear of the unknown and giving up what I did know. At that point, I made the decision for good or evil, for richer or for poorer, to go along with his strong leading.

Was it easy? Absolutely not! It was the hardest thing I ever did. I was sure we had made the biggest mistake of our lives. Did I immediately feel at home in Germany? No way! I got there physically in July, and my emotions arrived the next February. But in the end, I was glad I took the risk.

We committed to stay for three years, and we ended up staying almost ten. We now call those years the golden years for our family.

To be honest, if we had not been committed to each other and to God, if we had not felt there was a purpose in our lives and in our move to Europe that was larger than the two of us, and if we had not been committed to love, serve, and forgive each other, I honestly don't think we would have made it. But it was what we learned in those early years in Europe about ourselves, our marriage, and how to build spiritual intimacy that led us to develop our Marriage Alive Seminar and to found Marriage Alive International.

LIVING IT OUT

In Luke 10:27 we are challenged to love our neighbors as ourselves. This took on a fresh, new meaning when we applied it to our marriage. The word neighbor means the person closest to you. When you marry, your closest neighbor will be your spouse—the one you are choosing to share your life with at its deepest and most intimate level. If we love our partner as we love ourselves, we will have his or her best interest at heart, we will want to serve, not be served, and we will resist the urge to manipulate or pull power plays. We will have a relationship based on love and trust.

So many times conflict could be resolved if we just loved the other as we loved ourselves. Too often we are me-centered and want things to work out "my" way. But just the opposite approach is what promotes spiritual intimacy.

Unconditional Love and Acceptance

Central to our core belief system is a commitment to accept and love each other unconditionally—not "I'll love you if...," but "I'll love you in spite of. ..." However, this is not easy to do, and many times we come up short! In "real time" it is not always easy to accept each other. But in a spiritually intimate marriage, not only do we strive to accept one another, but we also strive to love each other unconditionally. Here is how the apostle Paul describes unconditional love in 1 Corinthians 13:4–7:

> *Love is patient, love is kind. It does not envy, it does not boast, it is not proud. It is not rude, it is not self-seeking, it is not easily angered, it keeps no records of wrongs. Love does not*

delight in evil but rejoices with the truth. It always protects, always trusts, always hopes, always perseveres.

Our love doesn't always match up with Paul's description. It's hard to love like that. It is certainly not natural and, in our experience, it's the spiritual dimension of life that empowers us to live out this kind of love with each other. We have to continually realize that love is a choice we can make.

Sometimes we give each other unconditional love in stressful times—like when Dave's migraine headache just wouldn't go away, and we had to cancel our dinner out. Claudia chose to pamper Dave, rather than complain. Or the time Claudia had a complicated root canal, and the dentist said, "Take a couple of aspirin when you get home, and you'll be just fine." Who was he kidding? Not Claudia! Through the throbbing pain that night Dave kept her supplied with ice packs and Jell-O. At other times our unconditional love has been very conditional, but we keep trying.

Consider the importance of unconditional love in the really hard times of life. I (Natelle) lay on the couch crying. I had just miscarried our first baby. Certain we would never be able to have children, I was depressed, angry, and devastated all at the same time. Curt could have retreated to his office, but instead he chose to stay home all day and sit quietly with me, hold me, wipe my tears away, and assure me. On that day, his unconditional love made the difference.

I (Curt) remember a turning point in my life when Natelle chose to trust me and give me her unconditional love and support. I wanted to leave a good, secure job with a Fortune 500 company to start my own business. She encouraged me and supported me even though it meant taking a big risk and signing a second mortgage on our house in order to secure a business loan. This happened when our children were both preschoolers and Natelle was a stay-at-home mom. We had no other income. It was this loan that put food on the table for the first two years of the business start-up. During such times of uncertainty and difficulty, her unconditional love and acceptance helped us get through the rough spots.

Forgiveness

When we fall short in accepting and loving each other unconditionally, we rely on another of our core values, which is being willing to forgive each other and ask for forgiveness. As God forgives us, we can forgive each other. A forgiving spirit helps us be more compassionate, tolerant, generous, and benevolent with each other. These traits help to build intimacy and trust in a marriage.

In the closeness of a marriage relationship, it is easy to become irritated and react negatively. Perhaps you are already experiencing some tension even before you say "I do." If little things already irritate you, do you assume you can deal with these after the wedding when the pressure is off? We have a better suggestion. Don't wait until then. Now is the time to develop the habit of forgiveness; however, you want to concentrate on your part, not what your partner has done.

In Matthew 7:3 we read, "Why do you look at the speck of sawdust in your *partner's* eye and pay no attention to the plank in your own eye?"[7] When we are upset, it is hard to focus on our own shortcomings, but first we need to get the plank out of our own eye before we criticize the other.

Matthew 7:4–5 continues, "How can you say to your [partner], 'Let me take the speck out of your eye,' when all the time there is a plank in your own eye? You hypocrite, first take the plank out of your own eye, and then you will see clearly to remove the speck from your [partner's] eye."

We suggest the following exercise. If presently you are not experiencing any irritations with your partner, we encourage you to learn this exercise for the future. You will need it if you want to develop spiritual intimacy in your marriage.

Step 1: List Your Partner's Shortcomings and Your Inappropriate Response

On a sheet of paper, make two columns. In the left column, list what your partner does that triggers a reaction in you. In the right column, list your inappropriate responses. Perhaps your partner is often late. Do you assume automatically that he or she just doesn't care or is trying to annoy you by not being punctual? What is your response? Do you lecture, sigh, or give the silent treatment? You may find that your responses are worse than what your partner did to trigger them. If so, admit your negative attitude and burn or tear up the paper. Do not show it to your partner! This exercise is for your benefit to help you get the plank out of your own eye!

Step 2: Admit Your Inappropriate Response and Attitude

You want to focus on your own inappropriate responses and attitudes, not what your partner did. Take responsibility for your own actions and reactions.

Step 3: Accept Your Partner with Strengths and Weaknesses as a Packaged Deal

Remember, your differences can complement each other, and unconditional acceptance should be one of your core values. You can't change another person; you can only change yourself. But when you concentrate on correcting your inappropriate responses and attitudes, wonderful things often happen. Others change in response to you. So don't waste time trying to change each other. Concentrate on being the person the other needs.

Step 4: Ask Forgiveness for Your Inappropriate Response

No relationship can thrive without forgiveness. No relationship is perfect; we all blow it from time to time. Relationships are like potted plants. The pot can be broken, but if the plant is repotted, if it is watered and given tender loving care, it will continue to grow and thrive. Forgiveness is a vital part of marriage. Without it, relationships die—like the potted plant left with its roots exposed. So if you need to ask for forgiveness, do it. If your partner asks you for forgiveness, give it. The director of a mental hospital said that half of his patients would be able to go home if they knew they were forgiven.

If you need to ask for forgiveness, here's a tip: Focus on what you have done wrong, not on the other's shortcomings. For example, say, "I was wrong to nag you about being late to the restaurant. Will you forgive me?" instead of saying, "I'm sorry I nagged you about being late, but you know you're wrong to always make us late!" Remember, you are pointing the finger at your inappropriate response. Don't use this moment as an opportunity to go on the attack. If you attack your partner, you're attacking your own future marriage partner.

Prayer

Another core belief that affects our level of spiritual intimacy is our commitment to practice the discipline of prayer. A unique spiritual resource in marriage is prayer. For us, praying together promotes spiritual closeness. In *To Understand Each Other,* well-known Swiss psychiatrist Dr. Paul Tournier wrote,

> Happy are the couples who do recognize and understand that their happiness is a gift of God, who can kneel together to express their thanks not only for the love which he has put in their hearts, the children he has given them or all of life's joys, but also for the progress in their marriage which he brings about through that hard school of mutual understanding.[8]

While kneeling together in prayer is a wonderful picture of spiritual intimacy, it is not always simple to do. Lane and Aaron are engaged. Both are relatively new in their faith. They want to grow together spiritually now and after their wedding, but at this point they are struggling with how to pray together. Lane said, "We want to pray together, but each time we try it turns into a disaster. I pray and then wait for Aaron to pray and all he says is 'Amen.'"

Aaron chimed in, "It's because Lane prays about everything. I can't get a word in edgewise and when she stops, I can't think of anything else to pray, so I just say, 'Amen.'"

They both looked at us (the Arps) for help. Our advice? We suggested that before they begin to pray, they make a list of things they want to pray about. Then each take turns praying as they pray through the list. That's what we did years ago when we began the habit of praying together. (In the beginning, we had the same problem as Lane and Aaron, but we won't tell you which one of us was the "wordy" one!)

If you are more of a private person and at this point aren't comfortable praying out loud, you might try taking a tip from our Quaker friends and try the Quaker method of sharing silence. This allows each of you to pray and worship according to your own personal needs, to seek communion with God separately and privately, yet be supported by the awareness that your partner is also sharing in the experience. It's an easy first step in praying and worshiping together. According to the Quaker tradition, the devotional time is appropriately concluded with the kiss of peace.[9]

Service

We believe that a shared life together must have a sacrificial quality, and this leads to service. First we try to serve each other. Jesus reminded us that he came to serve, not be served; that the first shall be last and the last shall be first; that it's better to give than to receive. Marriages would be revolutionized if we had a servant's heart and were committed to serving each other.

Second, we try to serve others. When we acknowledge that our life together is part of the divine purpose, we look for ways to live that out in service to others. We believe service promotes spiritual intimacy in a marriage relationship. Think of ways that together you can serve others. Maybe you would like to help serve at a soup kitchen, or go on a short-term missions project. Maybe you are concerned about ecology and taking better care of our world. Or perhaps you would like to help Habitat for Humanity build houses for people who need a place to live. Your own place of worship offers many opportunities for service. If you really want to serve others, you don't have to look very far to find those who desperately need your help! Every time we serve others together, our own marriage seems to benefit.

Don't wait until after you say "I do." Amber and Josh are a very giving couple and have spiced up their time of engagement by looking for ways to enjoy themselves as they serve others. Recently, they participated in the Race for the Cure, a fundraising benefit for breast cancer research. And on Thanksgiving they dressed in costumes to deliver Meals on Wheels to elderly shut-ins. Amber already had a Native American outfit, and Josh rented the appropriate pilgrim attire. After serving the meals, they went in costume to Josh's brother's home for a family dinner. They were a big hit even though some family members rolled their eyes. On this date, you might want to brainstorm together what you can do to serve others. It's easy to combine fun and service.

Now It's Your Turn

It is very difficult to talk about developing spiritual intimacy without sharing one's own journey. We've shared our journey with you in hopes it will motivate you to consider your own. Now it's your turn.

Turn to Date Nine in the Dating Guide and continue your journey toward spiritual intimacy together.

Date Ten

Choosing an Intentional Marriage

No more mischievous fallacy has ever been
propagated than the notion
that marriage requires no creative effort on the part
of those who enter it.
David and Vera Mace

*M*arriage is a choice, and we hope the last nine dates have helped you understand each other better so you can make wise choices in your relationship right now and in your marriage in the future. We hope we have helped you to visualize your future together more clearly and to answer the big questions, "Can I live with this other person for a lifetime?" "Do we have the skills and attitudes we need to build a successful marriage?" "Am I really ready to marry at this time?" Or, if you are seriously dating, "Am I ready to move forward to a deeper level of commitment?"

The real value of reexamining and reconfirming your decision to marry is that when you do marry, you can marry with confidence. You will be able to say with assurance, "Yes, I have chosen wisely." "Yes, our marriage will be one of the 50 percent of marriages that will last." So if you have any lingering concerns, now is the time to discuss them. This is also our last chance to encourage you to take advantage of other opportunities to prepare for your life together as husband and wife. Also, if you are ready to move forward with this relationship and you don't already have a mentor couple, let us encourage you to find one now. An older, seasoned couple will encourage you both now and after you say "I do."

CHOOSE YOUR INVOLVEMENT STYLE

How much intimacy and closeness do you desire for your marriage? Do you want to share life deeply with one another? Most couples would say "yes." To be loved, trusted, and appreciated, even when the other understands our weaknesses, gives us a sense of identity and self-confidence. Others desire less mutual involvement with each other. While every marriage is unique, most fit somewhere between these three involvement styles.

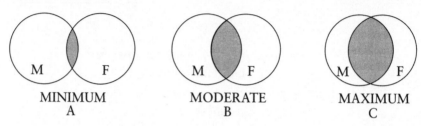

|MINIMUM|MODERATE|MAXIMUM|
|A|B|C|

The three illustrations represent three degrees of involvement in marriage.[1] Let's consider each.

Minimum Involvement (Illustration A)

In a minimum involvement marriage, the lives of the husband and wife overlap very little. They have separate interests and hobbies and are usually quite independent of each other.

Celia and Eric have been married for two years and have a minimum involvement marriage. Both have jobs requiring travel, but neither was aware of how separate their lives had become. Then one day they met accidentally in the Los Angeles airport. Neither even knew the other was supposed to be in California! They were incredulous. Celia said, "We looked at each other and realized that our circles were just too far apart."

Another couple, Lydia and Bill, actually live in different cities. Lydia's company recently relocated their office, and if she was going to keep her job, she had to move. Bill is just a couple of years from making partner at his law firm. Their decision? Lydia relocated with her company, and they connect on weekends. For us, that distance would be uncomfortable, but it seems to work for them.

Moderate Involvement (Illustration B)

Most marriages tend to fall in the moderate involvement range. Mike and Dianne work hard at keeping their circles overlapping at a moderate level. They are friends and lovers but also try to manage separate careers.

Soon after Dianne and Mike married, Mike, a graphic artist, had the opportunity to go into business for himself. He and Dianne spent many days and hours talking through the implications for their marriage and family. (They have two young children from Dianne's previous marriage.) They decided to go for it.

Mike's hours are long, and most weekends he has to finish an urgent project. Dianne's accounting job is not so stressful, though, and neither has a job that requires travel. Still, it's a real challenge to make their circles overlap at all. Rather than complain, they look for ways to work together to accomplish household projects. For instance, together they painted the outside of their house. They also designed a rock garden together and put up a fence in the backyard so their kids could play safely.

For Mike and Dianne, it's hard work to stay in the moderate involvement zone. The maximum level is just not realistic for them, and the minimum level is below their expectations for their marriage.

Maximum Involvement (Illustration C)

At this point in our lives, both of us couples have chosen a maximum involvement marriage style. We do seminars together, we write together, and most of our friends and hobbies are the same. We make most decisions together and share our innermost thoughts and dreams. We even have desks that face each other!

Our circles overlap to a great extent, although we still have interests and activities that do not include the other. Actually, we have to work on having a little separateness in our relationship. It's easy to have too much togetherness. Of course, couples can still have a maximum involvement relationship without working together. Perhaps they call or email several times a day to check in or consult on a decision, or their interests and friends are virtually identical—this also qualifies.

All three marriage styles are workable. In between these three styles is a wide range of varying shades and degrees of involvement. What style do you desire for your marriage? Do you agree on the level of mutual involvement for your future marriage?

In our seminars when we talk about the degrees of involvement in marriage, many couples realize how different their marriage is from what they really desire. Fortunately, marriage involvement styles are fluid, and it's possible to make a mid-course adjustment.

How Involved Do You Want to Be?

On Date Ten you will have the opportunity to talk about the degree of involvement you both desire for your upcoming marriage. Let us warn you, compromise will be part of the process.

Before John and Margaret were married, we (the Arps) guided them through ten similar dates. Each week they came to our home, and we talked about the date they had that week. It was fun to answer their questions and encourage them. We remember one week John and Margaret pulled into our driveway, but they didn't get out of the car. About thirty minutes later they knocked on the door. They had been discussing the degrees of involvement exercise in marriage and had had a heated argument.

Margaret wanted the maximum involvement, and John would be happy with minimum involvement. While not a pleasant experience, they were able to talk about it and adjust their expectations. John realized he would need to be a bit more involved, and Margaret realized that realistically they wouldn't be quite as involved as she would like to be.

Years later their marriage is still healthy and growing. Over the years their involvement style has varied. Margaret completed her college degree; they had two children; John attended seminary and is now the senior pastor of a large Denver suburban church. Recently we were leading our Marriage Alive seminar in their church, and they were reminiscing about their original ten dates and the marriage involvement exercise.

Margaret had the last word, "See, John, we really do have the maximum involvement style!"

The key to this part of your date is to realize that marriage is lived in seasons and in every season you will not experience the same degree of involvement. But what is critical is that you realize this and that you agree on what is possible during each season of your marriage.

CHOOSE TO MAKE TIME FOR EACH OTHER

According to a national survey, time is the number one problem that couples face in the first five years of marriage.[2] This is true whether it is a first marriage or a second marriage, with or without children. The challenge will be to find what works for you. But the bottom line is, if you're going to choose an intentional marriage, you will need to find time for each other.

Lucy and Ed recently married. For Ed, it's a second marriage. His first wife died in a tragic accident, leaving him with three small children. Ed, a publisher, met Lucy, a talented freelance writer, through his publishing company. They have been married for six months and are working hard to find an involvement style that works for them. Ed told us, "When I get home, we eat dinner. Then by the time we get the kids in bed and deliver the tenth glass of water, I have no energy left. Lucy often has a pressing editing deadline, and with the children, evenings are the best times for her to work."

"But we do try," Lucy said. "One evening last week we tried to watch a video on how to have a great marriage, and we both fell asleep! When we try to work on our relationship, we both get disappointed and give up. Where do we start?"

Our answer was to start with the time they did have. So the most important question is "What are you doing with the time you have?" Ed and Lucy had very little, but they did find some time. They now get up fifteen minutes earlier and start each day with a cup of coffee and a quiet time together. They also have hired a regular babysitter to come in one evening a week so they can have a date night.

Your marriage may start with less time pressures than Ed and Lucy's marriage, but regardless of what your circumstances will be, if you are going to spend time together, you will have to be intentional. And you won't just "find time." Finding time is circumstantial; making time is intentional. Let us give you some practical suggestions to help you capture time for each other after you are married. Consider the following four steps.[3]

Step 1: Make a Commitment

We have found that making time for each other has more to do with our attitude than our circumstances. We make time for those things that are the most important to us. To see what your priorities are, we suggest looking at what you presently do with your discretionary time and money. Remember, after you say "I do," you will need to be just as intentional about making time for each other. Step 2 will help you do just that.

Step 2: Analyze Your Current Time Constraints

We suggest that you keep a record for one week of how much time you spend at different activities. Then consider how much time is nondiscretionary. For instance, the hours you work are probably not very flexible. Next, list those things that must be done but the time frame for doing them is more flexible—household responsibilities, meal preparation, and so on. Now think about the discretionary things you do. How much time do you spend each week watching television and DVDs, reading the paper, golfing, playing tennis or racquetball, or surfing the Internet? How much time do you spend with family and friends?

Can you identify "time zappers"? What about television and DVDs? If you don't believe they are time zappers, just go into a video rental store on a Friday afternoon and observe all the people who are walking out loaded down with DVDs and videos. Paul Pearsall addresses this problem in *Super Marital Sex:* "TV addiction is one of the most detrimental influences on American marriages. It is a shared addiction, which is the worst type because it sometimes covertly robs the relationship of available time for intimacy, while both partners take unknowing part in the theft."[4]

Analyze the data you have collected; you will probably see blocks of time you can claim for your partner.

Step 3: Set Apart Time for Your Marriage

Set apart specific times dedicated to your partner. They may be short or long. Consider the following:

- *Five-second hugs and kisses.* Each time you leave and come home, claim five seconds to hug and kiss.
- *Ten minutes to share.* Have a ten-minute sharing time each day when you touch base with each other.
- *Weekly date nights.* A regular date night will help you be intentional about spending time together. If you're enjoying these dates, then we suggest our *10 Great Dates to Energize Your Marriage.*
- *Twenty-four-hour getaways.* Regular getaways will keep your marriage humming. Start the habit before you have children, and be determined not to stop it when the kids start coming.

(If you're marrying with children, we realize planning getaways will be more difficult, but please persevere! They're worth it!)

- *Candlelit dinners for two.* Start the habit right away of having romantic dinners twice a month.

Step 4: Guard Your Time

If you don't guard your time for each other, no one else will. When you are tempted to make a new time commitment, we suggest first asking, "Will what I'm about to commit myself to bring us closer together or put distance in our relationship?" "What will I drop if I add something else?" One of the most helpful things we ever learned how to do was to say no (to others, not to each other!).

From time to time you may want to take a hard look at how you spend your time and evaluate what activities you can easily eliminate from your schedule. Identifying what to let go is tough, because you don't want to disappoint a friend, relative, or coworker, but you need to learn to say no to activities that take up your time at the expense of your marriage relationship.

If you are getting too committed and need to pull back, ask yourself the following three questions. They will help you make hard choices.

1. *Is this activity essential?* Would the sky fall in if you didn't do this? For instance, you have to earn a living, eat, sleep, and so on.
2. *Is this activity really important?* Will it help you to be a better spouse? Maintaining a healthy diet, exercise, devotions and prayer, and regular dates enhances our relationship with each other, so they are important to us.
3. *Is this activity discretionary?* Is it optional, simply your choice, something you like to do? This might include civic and community activities or more personal things like watching television, staying after work on Friday evenings for social hour, or golfing.[5]

The key to making time for your marriage is to be honest about your needs and priorities and then be creative in how you approach your particular time constraints. The next important choice is to choose together to set goals for your marriage.

CHOOSE TO SET GOALS FOR YOUR MARRIAGE

We tell couples that if they want to have an intentional marriage, they will need to be intentional about setting some goals. Businesses thrive on goal setting, and marriages desperately need more of it! But few ever take the time to set specific objectives for their marriages, much less make a plan to accomplish them. Basically, a marriage goal is a target toward which you agree to work. You may want to look back over your ten dates and choose a few areas on which you would like to concentrate on, such as

1. understanding the ways we are different (Date Two).
2. improving our communication skills (Date Three).
3. learning to use the Speaker/Listener Technique and working on separating problem discussion from problem solution (Date Four).
4. setting financial goals and working out a budget (Date Five).
5. establishing a regular date night (Date Six).
6. keeping romance alive after we're married (Date Seven).
7. sharing household responsibilities (Date Eight).
8. establishing a devotional and prayer time together (Date Nine).

Obviously no one can work on all these goals at the same time. The next step is to choose one goal for the next few weeks. You may want to start in an area in which you can quickly see some progress. Then as you are encouraged by your success, go on to more difficult areas.

Getting Started

The next question is how to start. Three simple words will help you devise a plan of action: What? How? When?

What marriage goals have you chosen? Newlyweds Nicholas and Stacey chose to work on their communication skills.

How can you reach this goal? The answer to this question needs to be achievable and measurable so you will know when you get there. What activities would help Nicholas and Stacey accomplish their communications goal? Here's what they wrote:

1. We will repeat Dates Three and Four and review the skills we learned on those two dates.

2. We will practice identifying our communication patterns and attempt to use the connecting pattern.
3. We will each read a book on communication and discuss it.
4. We will not attack each other or defend ourselves! If we forget, the offender gets one warning. On the second offense, the offender will be the other's slave for thirty minutes.
5. We will start a daily ten-minute couple time.

When? Without answering this final question you will probably not reach your goal. This is the time to pull out your Blackberry, PDA, or calendar and indicate a time commitment for doing the above activities. For instance, Nicholas and Stacey set aside Tuesday nights to work on their communication. The first Tuesday night they had a bookstore date and picked out the book *A Lasting Promise* to read together. They choose ten minutes each morning before going to work to have their daily couple time.

Monitor Your Progress

What about interruptions? You can be sure they will appear, so it's important to monitor your progress. Be willing to flex when things don't go as planned. Unforeseeable things happen—an unexpected project deadline must be met, neighbors drop in, and so on. But even if you don't follow through with every activity or if you have to reschedule and reschedule them again, you will be closer to reaching your goal than if you had not planned at all. So be realistic, but also persevere.

That's what Nicholas and Stacey did. During the first month they had to reschedule two of their Tuesday night communication dates and found that some mornings were just too hectic for their ten-minute couple time. They flexed by having their couple time in the evening when they missed it in the morning.

When your planned date is interrupted, simply reschedule it. Be creative and flexible. You will find that as you begin to reach your goals you actually have an intentional marriage!

> *Now turn to Date Ten in your Dating Guide and get ready to have fun talking about how you are going to have an intentional marriage!*

Appendix

PREMARITAL INVENTORIES

A premarital inventory is an objective tool that gives you, as a couple, a look at how each of you perceives your unique relationship. It reveals how you agree and disagree on a variety of important relationship issues. It brings to light areas you need to discuss before marriage so that issues do not turn into major problems after marriage. This awareness will help you begin your marriage with more realistic expectations.

Will the inventory tell you if you should get married or not? No, that is a decision only you can make. The inventory is not a test with right or wrong answers that you pass or fail. Rather, it is an assessment instrument of 155–180 statements that help you learn more about yourself and your partner. Common inventory content categories include

- Marriage/Lifestyle Expectations
- Personality Issues
- Communication
- Problem-Solving
- Family of Origin
- Leisure Activities
- Sexual Expectations
- Children and Parenting
- Friends and Interests
- Role Relationships
- Religion and Values/Spiritual Beliefs
- Financial Issues/Money Management

Taking an inventory is a valuable investment of your time, energy, and emotion in building your relationship. Talk to your pastor, counselor, or mentor couple who is qualified to administer the inventory and who can facilitate reviewing the results with you. Two premarital inventories we highly recommend are

PREPARE Inventory:
Life Innovations, Inc.
P.O. Box 190
Minneapolis, MN 55440
Phone: 651-635-0511
www.lifeinnovations.com

FOCCUS Inventory:
FOCCUS, Inc.
3214 North 60th Street
Omaha, NE 68104
Phone: 402-551-9003
www.foccusinc.com

MARRIAGE SAVERS

Another good investment is Marriage Savers, which is a national nonprofit group that Harriet and Mike McManus created in 1996. It has worked with the clergy of 164 cities by September 2002 to create Community Marriage Policies (CMP) with the twin goals of pushing down the divorce rate and raising the marriage rate. Divorces have plunged in dozens of cities to date. For example the divorce rate is down 18 percent in three years in Tallahassee, and in only six years, down 29 percent in Austin. In two cities, divorces have been cut in half! In Kansas City the divorce rate has plunged 46 percent and a stunning 56 percent in Modesto, California. Its marriage rate is up 12 percent over sixteen years when U.S. marriages fell 18 percent.

Furthermore, when the clergy of a city create a CMP, Marriage Savers will train up to five Mentor Couples from each church along with the pastor, who in turn create a safety net under every marriage by training couples in the church on Friday and Saturday nights. Churches that train Mentor Couples can virtually eliminate divorce! For example, Killearn United Methodist Church in Tallahassee, with three thousand members, has trained a hundred couples for marriage, none of whom have divorced in four years, and the church has worked with twenty troubled marriages, losing only two to divorce. Some couples become Mentor Couples in marriage preparation, while "back-from-the-brink" couples are trained to help troubled marriages and those in stepfamilies to create Stepfamily Support Groups. Other couples are trained in a variety of strategies to enrich existing marriages, using materials such as the superb *10 Great Dates to Energize Your Marriage.*

Here is a proven way for churches and communities to declare "a new day for marriage and an old day for divorce." To learn more, see the website, www.marriagesavers.org, or call 301-469-5873.

Helpful Resources

Commitment

Stanley, Scott. *The Heart of Commitment*. Nashville: Nelson, 1998.

Communication

Stanley, Scott, Daniel Trathen, Savanna McCain, and Milt Bryan. *A Lasting Promise: A Christian Guide to Fighting for Your Marriage*. San Francisco: Jossey-Bass, 1998.

Markman, Howard J., Scott M. Stanley, Susan L. Blumberg. *Fighting for Your Marriage: Positive Steps for Preventing Divorce and Preserving a Lasting Love*. San Francisco: Jossey-Bass, 2001.

Dating

Arp, David, and Claudia Arp. *10 Great Dates to Energize Your Marriage*. Grand Rapids: Zondervan, 1997.

_____. *52 Dates for You and Your Mate*. Nashville: Nelson, 1993.

Finances

Jenkins, Natalie H., Scott M. Stanley, William C. Bailey, and Howard J. Markman. *You Paid How Much for That?: How to Win at Money without Losing at Love*. San Francisco: Jossey-Bass, 2002.

Gender Differences

Clarke, David. *Men Are Clams, Women Are Crowbars: Understand Your Differences and Make Them Work*. Uhrichsville, OH: Promise Press, 1998.

Farrell, Bill, and Pam Farrell. *Men Are Like Waffles, Women Are Like Spaghetti*. Eugene, OR: Harvest House, 2001.

Gray, John. *Men Are from Mars, Women Are from Venus: A Practical Guide for Improving Communication and Getting What You Want in Your Relationship*. New York: HarperCollins, 1992.

Harley, Willard F. Jr. *His Needs, Her Needs: Building an Affair-Proof Marriage*. Grand Rapids: Revell, 1986.

Leman, Kevin. *Making Sense of the Men in Your Life: What Makes Them Tick, What Ticks You off, and How to Live in Harmony*. Nashville: Nelson, 2000.

Pease, Barbara, and Allan Pease. *Why Men Don't Listen and Women Can't Read Maps: How We're Different and What to Do about It.* New York: Broadway Books, 2000.

Rosberg, Gary, and Barbara Rosberg. *The 5 Love Needs of Men and Women.* Wheaton, IL: Tyndale House, 2000.

General Marriage

Chapman, Gary. *The Five Love Languages: How to Express Heartfelt Commitment to Your Mate.* Chicago: Northfield, 1995.

Clinton, Tim, and Julie Clinton. *The Marriage You've Always Wanted: How to Grow a Stronger, More Intimate Relationship.* Nashville: Nelson, 2000.

Cloud, Henry, and John Townsend. *Boundaries in Marriage.* Grand Rapids: Zondervan, 1999.

Gottman, John M., and Joan DeClaire. *The Relationship Cure: A 5 Step Guide for Building Better Connections with Family, Friends, and Lovers.* New York: Crown, 2001.

Gottman, John M., and Nan Silver. *The Seven Principles for Making Marriage Work.* New York: Crown, 1999.

Harley, Willard F. *Fall in Love, Stay in Love.* Grand Rapids: Revell, 2001.

Littauer, Florence, and Fred Littauer. *After Every Wedding Comes a Marriage.* Eugene, OR: Harvest House, 1997.

Littauer, Marita, and Chuck Noon. *Love Extravagantly: Making Modern Marriage Work.* Minneapolis: Bethany House, 2001.

Olson, David H., and Amy K. Olson. *Empowering Couples: Building on Your Strengths.* Minneapolis: Life Innovations, 2000.

Parrott, Les, III, and Leslie Parrott. *Saving Your Marriage Before It Starts: Seven Questions to Ask Before (and After) You Marry.* Grand Rapids: Zondervan, 1995.

Piver, Susan. *The Hard Questions: 100 Essential Questions to Ask Before You Say "I Do."* New York: Penguin Putnam, 2000.

Smalley, Gary. *Hidden Keys of a Loving Lasting Marriage.* Grand Rapids: Zondervan, 1988.

Smalley, Gary. *Making Love Last Forever.* Dallas: Word, 1996.

Smalley, Gary, and John Trent. *Love Is a Decision: Proven Techniques to Keep Your Marriage Alive and Lively.* Dallas: Word, 1989.

Smalley, Gary, and John Trent. *The Language of Love: A Powerful Way to Maximize Insight, Intimacy, and Understanding.* Wheaton, IL: Tyndale, 1991.

Smalley, Gary, and John Trent. *The Two Sides of Love: Using Personality Strengths to Greatly Improve Your Relationships.* Wheaton, IL: Tyndale, 1990.

Waite, Linda J., and Maggie Gallagher. *The Case for Marriage: Why Married People Are Happier, Healthier, and Better Off Financially.* New York: Doubleday, 2000.

Wallerstein, Judith S., and Sandra Blakeslee. *The Good Marriage: How and Why Love Lasts.* New York: Houghton Mifflin, 1995.

Wright, H. Norman, and Wes Roberts. *Before You Say "I Do": A Marriage Preparation Manual for Couples.* Eugene, OR: Harvest House, 1997.

Wright, H. Norman. *So You're Getting Married: The Keys to Building a Strong, Lasting Relationship.* Ventura, CA: Regal, 1985.

Sexuality

Arp, David, and Claudia Arp. *Love Life for Parents: How to Have Kids and a Sex Life Too.* Grand Rapids: Zondervan, 1998.

Penner, Clifford L., and Joyce J. Penner. *Getting Your Sex Life off to a Great Start: A Guide for Engaged and Newlywed Couples.* Dallas: Word, 1994.

Penner, Clifford, and Joyce Penner. *Men and Sex.* Nashville: Nelson, 1997.

Penner, Clifford, and Joyce Penner. *The Gift of Sex: A Guide to Sexual Fulfillment.* Dallas: Word, 1981.

Leman, Kevin. *Sex Begins in the Kitchen.* Grand Rapids: Revell, 1999.

Rosenau, Douglas E. *A Celebration of Sex: A Guide to Enjoying God's Gift of Married Sexual Pleasure.* Nashville: Nelson, 1994.

Wheat, Ed, and Gaye Wheat. *Intended for Pleasure: Sex Technique and Sexual Fulfillment in Christian Marriage.* Grand Rapids: Revell, 1977.

Wheat, Ed, and Gloria Okes Perkins. *Love Life for Every Married Couple: How to Fall in Love, Stay in Love, Rekindle Your Love.* Grand Rapids: Zondervan, 1980.

Spirituality

Arp, David, and Claudia Arp. *Marriage Moments.* Ann Arbor, MI: Servant Publications, 1998.

_____. *Quiet Whispers from God's Heart for Couples.* Nashville: Countryman, Nelson, 1999.

God's Words of Life on Marriage. Grand Rapids: Zondervan, 2000.

Marriage Devotional Bible. Grand Rapids: Zondervan, Grand Rapids: Zondervan, 2000.

Stoop, David, and Jan Stoop. *When Couples Pray Together: Creating Intimacy and Spiritual Wholeness.* Ann Arbor, MI: Vine Books, 2000.

Williamson, Martha. *Inviting God to Your Wedding.* New York: Harmony Books, 2000.

Notes

Welcome to Your 10 Great Dates

1. For information about PREPARE and FOCCUS see Appendix 1

2. Rudy and Faith Buettner, Mentors' Guide for FOCCUS (Potomac, MD: Marriage Savers, 1999). During mentoring sessions, the mentor couple help the engaged couple talk through issues on which they agree or disagree and help them learn skills that will enable them to build a successful marriage. After they are married, the mentor couple is available to give encouragement and to help the newlyweds get off to a good start. For more information about the Marriage Savers mentoring program see Appendix 2 and visit www.marriagesavers.org.

Date One—Sharing Hopes, Dreams, and Expectations

1. Dr. Barbara Markey, founder of the FOCCUS inventory, states that the expectation that one can change his or her mate after marriage relates to the fact that the highest divorce rate is in the first three years of marriage. A large part of a "good match" is understanding the match and deciding if they can live and grow with it. Her findings of the percentages of engagements that do not result in marriage are from the Creighton University Time, Sex and Money Study on the first five years of marriage.

Date Two—Appreciating Your Differences

1. Howard Markman, Scott Stanley, and Susan L. Blumberg, *Fighting for Your Marriage* (San Francisco: Jossey-Bass Publishers, 2001), 69, 28.

Date Three—Communicating and Connecting

1. We are grateful to David and Vera Mace for their input into our lives and marriage and for the excellent training we received from the Association of Couples in Marriage Enrichment (A.C.M.E.) Training Workshops with them. Our basic philosophy of the three patterns of communication and how to deal with anger and conflict is adapted from our training with the Maces and used with their permission. A.C.M.E. offers excellent leadership training for those interested in leading marriage enrichment groups. For more information about A.C.M.E. visit www.bettermarriages.org.

2. We first learned the concept of the feelings formula in 1977 from Bill and Kathy Clarke, who for years have conducted Marriage and Family Enrichment Institutes. We met the Clarkes when we were just beginning

our work in marriage enrichment, and their input over the years has enriched our own work in marriage and family enrichment.

Date Four—Solving Problems as a Couple

1. We thank Doug Wilson for sharing his illustration of animal characters with us in Vienna, Austria, in 1981, and giving us permission to adapt his concept for use in our work in marriage enrichment. Doug and his wife, Karen, spent several days with us when we were first designing our Marriage Alive seminar and gave strategic input that has benefited us and many other couples through the years.

2. Howard Markman, Scott Stanley, and Susan L. Blumberg, *Fighting for Your Marriage* (San Francisco: Jossey-Bass Publishers, 2001), 76.

3. John M. Gottman, Ph.D., *The Seven Principles for Making Marriage Work* (New York: Three Rivers Press, 1999), 129–130.

4. Markman, Stanley, and Blumberg, *Fighting for Your Marriage*, 110–12. Used by permission. To order *Fighting for Your Marriage* books, audio, or video tapes: Call 1-800-366-0166. Copyright by PREP Educational Products, Inc., 1991.

5. Our four steps for resolving conflict were originally adapted from H. Norm Wright's book, *The Pillars of Marriage* (Glendale, CA: Regal, 1979), 158. This is just one of Norm Wright's many excellent marriage enrichment resources. We wish to express our deep appreciation to Norm for his influence in not only our lives and work but many others as well.

Date Five—Managing Your Money

1. Karen S. Peterson, "Adults Should Know Status of Parents," *USA Today* (March 12, 1992).

2. Markey, *Time, Sex and Money: The First Five Years of Marriage* (Omaha: Center for Marriage and Family, Creighton University, 2000), 72.

3. David H. Olson, *Empowering Couples* (Minneapolis: Study Life Innovations, 2000), 91.

4. Natalie Jenkins, Scott Stanley, William Bailey, and Howard Markman, *You Paid How Much for That?* (San Francisco: Jossey-Bass, 2002), 43.

5. M. Scott Peck, *The Road Less Traveled* (New York: Walker, 1985), 3.

6. Barbara Markey, FOCCUS Facilitator Notebook, (Omaha: FOCCUS, Inc., 2000), 71.

Date Six—Leaving and Cleaving

1. David and Vera Mace, *When the Honeymoon's Over* (Nashville: Abingdon Press, 1988), adapted from pages 84–87.

2. Ibid., 87, 88.

3. Scott Stanley, *The Heart of Commitment* (Nashville: Nelson, 1998), 4.

4. John Gottman, *Why Marriages Succeed or Fail* (New York: Simon and Schuster, 1994), 29.

Date Seven—Celebrating Intimacy, Love, and Romance

1. Scott Stanley, et al., *A Lasting Promise* (San Francisco: Jossey-Bass, 1998), 149.

2. The Facets of a Love Life are adapted from: David and Claudia Arp, *Love Life for Parents* (Grand Rapids: Zondervan, 1998), 22–31.

3. Les and Leslie Parrott, *Saving Your Second Marriage Before It Starts* (Grand Rapids: Zondervan, 2001), 56, 57.

4. Judith Wallerstein and Sandra Blakeslee, *The Good Marriage* (New York: Houghton Mifflin, 1995), 192.

5. Howard Markman, Scott Stanley, and Susan L. Blumberg, *Fighting for Your Marriage* (San Francisco: Jossey-Bass Publishers, 2001), 232–33.

6. Ibid., 231.

7. Email from Barbara Markey on March 3, 2002.

Date Eight—Realizing Roles and Planning for Family

1. Olson, *Empowering Couples* (Minneapolis: Study Life Innovations, 2001), 79.

Date Nine—Developing Spiritual Intimacy

1. Olson, *Empowering Couples* (Minneapolis: Study Life Innovations, 2001), 113.

2. Les and Leslie Parrott, *Saving Your Marriage Before It Starts* (Grand Rapids: Zondervan, 1995), 145.

3. Markman, Stanley, and Blumberg, *Fighting for Your Marriage,* 285.

4. Paul Pearsall, *Super Marital Sex* (New York: Ivy Books, 1987), 217.

5. Scott Stanley, et al., *A Lasting Promise* (San Francisco: Jossey-Bass, 1998), 261.

6. Les and Leslie Parrott, *Saving Your Marriage Before It Starts* (Grand Rapids: Zondervan, 1995), 135.

7. Our paraphrase.

8. Paul Tournier, *To Understand Each Other* (Atlanta: John Knox, 1967), 60.

9. David and Vera Mace, *What's Happening to Clergy Marriages?* (Nashville: Abingdon, 1980), 103–4.

Date Ten—Choosing an Intentional Marriage

1. David Mace and Vera Mace, *We Can Have Better Marriages If We Really Want Them* (Nashville: Abingdon, 1974), 76.

2. Markey, *Time, Sex and Money: The First Five Years of Marriage* (Omaha: Center for Marriage and Family, Creighton University, 2000), 72.

3. The four steps are adapted from David and Claudia Arp, *Love Life for Parents* (Grand Rapids: Zondervan, 1998), 89–93.

4. Paul Persall, *Super Marital Sex* (New York: Ivy books, 1987).

5. Arp and Arp, *Love Life for Parents,* 100.

About the Authors

Claudia Arp and David Arp, MSW, a husband-wife team, are founders and directors of Marriage Alive International, a groundbreaking ministry dedicated to providing resources and training to empower churches to help build better marriages and families. Their Marriage Alive seminar is popular across the United States and in Europe.

The Arps are popular conference speakers, columnists, and authors of numerous books and video curricula including *10 Great Dates to Energize Your Marriage, Love Life for Parents, Empty Nesting,* and the Gold Medallion Award-winning *The Second Half of Marriage.* Frequent contributors to print and broadcast media, the Arps have appeared as empty nest experts on the NBC *Today Show,* CBS *This Morning,* and Focus on the Family. Their work has been featured in publications such as *USA Today, The Christian Science Monitor, Reader's Digest New Choices Magazine, Marriage Partnership,* and *Focus on the Family Magazine.*

David and Claudia have been married for over thirty-five years, have three married sons and seven grandchildren, and live in Knoxville, Tennessee.

Curt Brown and Natelle Brown are Directors of Marriage Ministry at Wellshire Presbyterian Church in Denver, Colorado, and advisors to the Rocky Mountain Family Council Colorado Marriage Project. They are developers and leaders of the Marriage Alive Before You Say "I Do" Seminar and also lead Marriage Alive and Second Half of Marriage Seminars.

The Browns met and married in college where both earned B.A. degrees in Business Administration, and Natelle completed a second major in Home Economics. Curt worked for a Fortune 500 company and in 1982 cofounded a computer software company. In 1998, Curt sold his interest in the business to his partners, and after many years as a stay-at-home mom, Natelle completed her M.A. degree in Marriage and Family Therapy.

At that point Curt and Natelle began working together in a marriage ministry devoted to mentoring soon-to-be-married couples as well as working with marrieds. In 2000, the Browns joined the staff of Marriage Alive. As marriage educators, coaches, and mentors, Curt and Natelle have a passion for helping seriously dating and engaged couples prepare for marriage and equipping married couples to build, strengthen, and enrich their relationships. The Browns have been married twenty-nine years, have two adult children, and live in the foothills of the Rocky Mountains.

About Marriage Alive International, Inc

Marriage Alive International, Inc., founded by husband-wife team Claudia Arp and David Arp, MSW, is a nonprofit marriage and family enrichment ministry dedicated to providing resources, seminars, and training to empower churches to help build better marriages and families. Marriage Alive also works with community organizations, the U.S. military, schools, and businesses.

The Arps are marriage and family educators and have been involved in marriage ministry in the USA and in Europe for more than twenty-five years. Their Marriage Alive seminar is popular across the U.S. and in Europe. In 2000, Curt and Natelle Brown joined Marriage Alive. As marriage educators, coaches, and mentors, Curt and Natelle have a passion for helping seriously dating and engaged couples prepare for marriage and equipping married couples to build, strengthen, and enrich their relationships.

The Vision of Marriage Alive is to see a movement of trained and equipped couples working through congregations and other established communities to transform marriage and family relationships.

The Mission of Marriage Alive is to identify, train, and empower leaders who invest in others by building strong marriage and family relationships through the integration of biblical truth, contemporary research, practical application, and fun.

Our Resources and Services

• Marriage and family books in seven languages

• Video-based educational programs including *10 Great Dates to Energize Your Marriage* and *Second Half of Marriage*

• Marriage, pre-marriage, and parenting seminars including *Before You Say "I Do," Marriage Alive, Second Half of Marriage,* and *Empty Nesting* seminars

• Consulting, training, leadership development, coaching, and mentoring

Contact Marriage Alive at www.marriagealive.com or (888) 690–6667.

10 Great Dates to Energize Your Marriage

David and Claudia Arp

Dating doesn't have to be only a memory or just another boring evening at the movies. David and Claudia Arp have revolutionized dating by creating Couples' Nights Out memory-making evenings built on key, marriage-enriching themes. This approach to relationship growth involves both partners, is low-key, and best of all, is exciting, proven, and fun!

This book is organized around ten great dates that couples will experience to energize their marriage with fun, intimacy, and romance.

Learn how to communicate better, build a creative sex life, process anger and resolve conflicts, develop spiritual intimacy, balance busy lifestyles and more!

"*10 Great Dates* is a simple and practical plan, sure to revive romance and rejuvenate the fun quotient in your marriage."

—Les and Leslie Parrott, authors of
Saving Your Marriage Before It Starts

Softcover: 978-0-310-21091-7

Pick up a copy today at your favorite bookstore!

10 Great Dates to Energize Your Marriage

The Best Tips from the Marriage Alive Seminars

David and Claudia Arp

10 Great Dates has such great appeal to couples in any setting. From small to large groups, for retreats or personal use, 10 Great Dates is an exciting, proven program that is low-key, effective, easy-to-lead, and husband-friendly. Combining fun dates and marriage education skills, this video curriculum gives couples time-out to build their marriage and enrich their relationship.

Designed for use with the book *10 Great Dates to Energize Your Marriage* as the participant's guide, this curriculum has everything you need to launch your group (or just the two of you) on your great dates. Leading your group is as easy as plugging in the coffee pot and DVD player and letting the Arps take it from there. You'll love growing together while going out together!

10 Great Dates includes:

- DVD with ten video sessions to launch your dates
- PDF files with a customizable press release, sample brochure, and certificate of completion are contained on the DVD
- Thirty-two-page Leader's Guide

"10 Great Dates™ is definitely the most widely used marriage education program. It is being used by all denominations, by the military, and by other groups around the country."

—Diane Sollee, MSW, founder and director,
SmartMarriages.com

DVD: 978-0-310-27136-9

The Second Half of Marriage

Facing the Eight Challenges of Every Long-Term Marriage

David and Claudia Arp

David and Claudia Arp help empty-nesters overcome eight marital challenges to make the rest of their marriage the best of their marriage.

Your children are gone or leaving soon. It's time to focus once again on your own future and especially on your marriage. What's in store for the second half? David and Claudia Arp provide answers and practical help in this groundbreaking book. Drawing on their national survey of hundreds of "second-half" couples, the Arps reveal eight marital challenges every long-term marriage faces, and they offer strategies and exercises for meeting each of them. *The Second Half of Marriage* will challenge you to create a vision for the rest of your life together — and inspire you to make that vision a reality.

"The Arps's *Second Half of Marriage* is a critical resource everyone needs to prepare for the empty nest."
—H. Norman Wright, author of *Before You Say "I Do":*
A Marriage Preparation Manual for Couples

Softcover: 978-0-310-21935-4

Pick up a copy today at your favorite bookstore!

Suddenly They're 13

The Art of Hugging a Cactus

David and Claudia Arp

This book helps parents and adolescents make a positive transition into the teenage years and then keep talking and relating to each other as teens moves toward adulthood.

What do you do when that huggable son or daughter suddenly sprouts needles? Trusted family life educators and seminar leaders David and Claudia Arp help frustrated parents discover the secrets of communicating with their teenage "cactus." Through the "four Rs" of regrouping, releasing, relating, and relaxing, the Arps help parents launch their almost-thirteen into the teen years, using the Teenage Challenge and yearly Birthday Boxes. Other topics include choosing "majors and minors," promoting spiritual growth, and communicating when things have gone wrong. *Suddenly They're 13* is the textbook for parents who are serious about growing responsible and caring adults.

> "What a positive and practical approach to parenting teens! I love the action steps for encouraging teenagers and preparing them for life in the adult world. The ideas will be easy to pass on to parents of teens at my church, and I'm now better prepared for my own children to suddenly turn thirteen!"
>
> —Doug Fields, youth pastor, Saddleback Church and author of *Purpose Driven™ Youth Ministry*

Softcover: 978-0-310-22788-7

Pick up a copy today at your favorite bookstore!

10 Great Dates for Empty Nesters

David and Claudia Arp

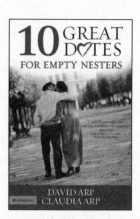

A simple dating plan that is sure to revive romance and rejuvenate the fun quotient in your empty-nest marriage

It's just the two of you again and it's time to renew your relationship. You can reconnect and reclaim that same spark, excitement, and creativity you experienced before you had kids through ten innovative, fun dates guaranteed to spice up your marriage. Specially crafted for empty-nesters, these dates are based on marriage-enriching themes, such as

- Becoming a couple again
- Rediscovering intimate talk
- Revitalizing your love life
- Growing together spiritually
- Relating to adult children
- Becoming best friends

10 Great Dates for Empty Nesters will fill your empty nest with fun, friendship, and romance. It is refreshing to read a book about marriage written by people who don't just believe in marriage but actually understand how it works.

—John Gray, Author, *Men Are from Mars, Women Are from Venus*

Softcover: 978-0-310-25656-4

Pick up a copy today at your favorite bookstore!

ZONDERVAN®
.com

Part Two

Your 10 Great Dates Dating Guide

Your Dating Plan

Write in when you are going to have each date!

Date One: Sharing Hopes, Dreams, and Expectations
   is scheduled for _____

Date Two: Appreciating Your Differences
   is scheduled for _____

Date Three: Communicating and Connecting
   is scheduled for _____

Date Four: Solving Problems as a Couple
   is scheduled for _____

Date Five: Managing Your Money
   is scheduled for _____

Date Six: Leaving and Cleaving
   is scheduled for _____

Date Seven: Celebrating Intimacy, Love, and Romance
   is scheduled for _____

Date Eight: Realizing Roles and Planning for Family
   is scheduled for _____

Date Nine: Developing Spiritual Intimacy
   is scheduled for _____

Date Ten: Choosing an Intentional Marriage
   is scheduled for _____

Your Dating Ground Rules

To get the most out of each date we make the following suggestions:

- *Read the corresponding chapter and/or the chapter summary.* If you have not filled out the exercise, do so before you begin your discussion.
- *Stay positive!* This is not the time to tell the other what he or she has done wrong.
- *Be future focused.* Focus on what you want your relationship to be like in the future. Don't concentrate on past failures. (It's okay to remember past successes.)
- *Talk about your relationship.* Do not talk about your job, future in-laws, or wedding details unless it's part of the topic of the date. Now is the time to plan your life together.
- *Give a gift of love.* Some topics will excite you more than others. On the less exciting ones, give a gift of love. Participate enthusiastically!
- *Don't force it.* If you get on a negative track, stop that discussion. Move on to another topic that you both feel good about.
- *If you get stuck, ask for help.* If during your dates an issue comes up that you can't handle together, talk to your pastor, mentor couple, or counselor.
- *Use good communication skills.* Be prepared for some surprises and new insights about each other. They can open new opportunities for growth and intimacy in your relationship. Following are several tips for sharing your answers:

  1. Be honest, yet never unkind.
  2. Remember to start your sentences with "I" and let them reflect back on you.
  3. Resist attacking the other or defending yourself.
  4. Try to use the feelings formula.
  5. Be specific and positive.

- *Have fun!* Remember why you are considering getting married in the first place. Also think about why you are dating. It is to enrich your relationship as you prepare for the future.
- *After each date, take the post-date application tips seriously!* Remember you are developing healthy habits that will enrich your life together long after your *10 Great Dates* are completed.

Date One

Sharing Hopes, Dreams, and Expectations

Date One will help you look at your expectations and consider which ones are realistic.

PRE-DATE PREPARATION

- Read chapter 1, "Sharing Hopes, Dreams, and Expectations."
- Read through the Date One Exercise and take notes. Looking over the exercise before your date gives time for reflection. Also, if one of you is more verbal than the other, making a few notes will give you time to formulate your thoughts.
- Make reservations at a favorite restaurant. (The one making the reservations may want to let the place be a surprise for the other.)
- If applicable, make arrangements for child care.
- Think about what you will wear. Choose an outfit you think the other would like. Remember, this is a date!

DATE NIGHT TIPS

- Plan to use the whole evening. Don't think about rushing home to watch your favorite TV program. If there is something you want to watch, use your VCR and record it for another evening.
- During a leisurely dinner, talk through the dating exercises. Part 1 will help you look at your expectations and compare them with your partner's.
- Parts 1 and 2 will help you focus on your hopes, dreams, and expectations for the future.
- Before you start, review communication tips in the Dating Ground Rules, page 162.

CHAPTER SUMMARY

If you are engaged or seriously considering marriage, this date will help you look at your hopes, dreams, and expectations. Do you expect your partner to change some of his/her ways after you marry? Too many who are planning marriage believe this. The value of these dates and other marriage preparation resources is having the opportunity to reexamine and reconfirm your decision to marry. You can start that process by looking realistically at your expectations. In our national survey of long-term marriages, we found three common strands in those marriages that are alive and healthy: (1) They put their relationship first, (2) both spouses are committed to growing together, and (3) they work at staying close. As you enjoy your memories and look at your relationship as it is now, you will be better equipped to share your expectations for the future. Enjoy your first great date!

POST-DATE APPLICATION

- Look for ways to compliment each other between now and the next date. Give at least one honest compliment each day—in person or by phone or email.
- Continue to share your hopes and dreams (Part 2).

> *Bonus Date: Go to a Parade of Homes or other open houses and discuss your likes and dislikes and dream about your future home together.*

Date One Exercise

PART 1: EXPECTATION SURVEY[1]

What are your expectations? As you consider marriage, what is most important to you and your partner? Rate these eight areas on a scale of 1 to 5 (1 being not so important and 5 being very important). Now rate them as you think your partner would rate them. Compare your lists and discuss.

____ 1. *Commitment and Security*—The knowledge of permanence and dedication in the relationship; financial and material well-being.

____ 2. *Companionship and Friendship*—Having a friend who goes through all the joys and sorrows of life with you, a soul partner; having common areas of interest.

____ 3. *Sexuality and Sensuality*—Experiencing physical intimacy, romance, and love in marriage; the pleasure of a growing love relationship.

____ 4. *Affection and Tenderness*—Experiencing regularly the touch, the kiss, the winks across the room that say, "I love you," "I care," and "I'm thinking of you."

____ 5. *Encouragement*—Having verbal support and appreciation of your work and efforts in your profession, in your home, and so on.

____ 6. *Intellectual Closeness*—Discussing and growing together in common areas of intellectual thought.

____ 7. *Mutual Activity*—Doing things together such as politics, sports, church work, and hobbies.

____ 8. *Building a Family*—Having a family and parenting together.

Which of the above could I never live without?

Which would I be okay without?

---

[1]Expectation Survey was adapted from: Mary Susan Miller, "What are Your Expectations from Marriage?" *Family Life Today* (October 1980), 19.

PART 2: SHARING HOPES, DREAMS, AND EXPECTATIONS

Pick two or three topics you would like to talk about and have fun sharing your hopes, dreams, and expectations!

- Where you would like to live

- Your ideal home

- Career plans and goals

- Finances

- Family traditions and holiday celebrations

- Your dream getaway

- Spirituality

- Your future family

- Short-term and long-term goals

- Other

Date One Exercise

PART 1: EXPECTATION SURVEY[1]

What are your expectations? As you consider marriage, what is most important to you and your partner? Rate these eight areas on a scale of 1 to 5 (1 being not so important and 5 being very important). Now rate them as you think your partner would rate them. Compare your lists and discuss.

__ __ 1. *Commitment and Security*—The knowledge of permanence and dedication in the relationship; financial and material well-being.

__ __ 2. *Companionship and Friendship*—Having a friend who goes through all the joys and sorrows of life with you, a soul partner; having common areas of interest.

__ __ 3. *Sexuality and Sensuality*—Experiencing physical intimacy, romance, and love in marriage; the pleasure of a growing love relationship.

__ __ 4. *Affection and Tenderness*—Experiencing regularly the touch, the kiss, the winks across the room that say, "I love you," "I care," and "I'm thinking of you."

__ __ 5. *Encouragement*—Having verbal support and appreciation of your work and efforts in your profession, in your home, and so on.

__ __ 6. *Intellectual Closeness*—Discussing and growing together in common areas of intellectual thought.

__ __ 7. *Mutual Activity*—Doing things together such as politics, sports, church work, and hobbies.

__ __ 8. *Building a Family*—Having a family and parenting together.

Which of the above could I never live without?

Which would I be okay without?

---

[1]Expectation Survey was adapted from: Mary Susan Miller, "What are Your Expectations from Marriage?" *Family Life Today* (October 1980), 19.

PART 2: SHARING HOPES, DREAMS, AND EXPECTATIONS

Pick two or three topics you would like to talk about and have fun sharing your hopes, dreams, and expectations!

- Where you would like to live

- Your ideal home

- Career plans and goals

- Finances

- Family traditions and holiday celebrations

- Your dream getaway

- Spirituality

- Your future family

- Short-term and long-term goals

- Other

10 Great Dates Before You Say "I Do" (Zondervan).
© 2003 David and Claudia Arp, Curt and Natelle Brown. Illegal to copy.

Date Two

Appreciating Your Differences

The purpose of this date is to give you the opportunity to consider how you can benefit from each other's strengths and how you can complement each other in the ways you are different.

PRE-DATE PREPARATION

- Read chapter 2, "Appreciating Your Differences."
- Preview the Date Two Exercise.
- Plan to go to your favorite hangout. Choose a place where you can talk privately.

DATE NIGHT TIPS

- While discussing "Balancing Your Seesaws," concentrate on each other's strengths.
- Making a list of your couple strengths will help you appreciate how you fill each other's gaps.

CHAPTER SUMMARY

Have you heard the old adage, "Opposites attract"? If this is true in your experience and if you want to have a great relationship, you will need to learn how to appreciate your differences. On this date you will look at seven continuums that illustrate some human polarities. As you look at each continuum, think about your relationship. Both sides of each continuum have strengths and weaknesses. Which side you are on is less important than understanding that people are different. To build a strong marriage you will need to learn how to benefit from the ways you are alike and the ways you are different. Your different strengths can help you balance each other—especially if you appreciate those differences and don't feel threatened by them. In areas where you have similar strengths, you may need to look for ways to work together harmoniously.

POST-DATE APPLICATION

- Look for ways you are different that complement each other.
- In ways that you are alike, look for ways you can compensate.
- Affirm your partner's positive characteristics.

> *Bonus date: Go to a video store, separate, and each pick a movie of your choice. How different are the movies?*

Date Two Exercise

BALANCING YOUR SEESAWS

Place yourself and your partner on each continuum.

Feelings-Oriented   Facts-Oriented

Private   Public

Spontaneous   Planner

Live-Wire   Laid-Back

Night Owl   Day Lark

Time-Oriented   Not Time-Oriented

Saver   Spender

In looking at each seesaw discuss the following questions:

1. If you are opposites, how can you complement each other?

2. If you are like, how can you compensate?

3. List other ways in which you are alike or opposite.

4. Make a list of your combined strengths. These are the strengths of your potential marriage partnership!

Date Two Exercise

BALANCING YOUR SEESAWS

Place yourself and your partner on each continuum.

Feelings-Oriented	Facts-Oriented

Private	Public

Spontaneous	Planner

Live-Wire	Laid-Back

Night Owl	Day Lark

Time-Oriented	Not Time-Oriented

Saver	Spender

In looking at each seesaw discuss the following questions:

1. If you are opposites, how can you complement each other?

2. If you are alike, how can you compensate?

3. List other ways in which you are alike or opposite.

4. Make a list of your combined strengths. These are the strengths of your potential marriage partnership!

Date Three

Communicating and Connecting

This date will help you connect through sharing your feelings with one another and by talking about your family of origin's communication style.

PRE-DATE PREPARATION

- Read chapter 3, "Communicating and Connecting."
- Review the Date Three Exercise.
- Choose a location that will allow you to talk quietly—perhaps a picnic in a park or a bookstore with a coffee shop.

DATE NIGHT TIPS

- Discuss your exercise, alternating who goes first.
- Be prepared for some new insights into your partner.
- Review communication tips in Dating Ground Rules, page 162.
- IMPORTANT: Stay positive. If conflicts arise in the conversation, note them and save them for later; don't discuss them now!

CHAPTER SUMMARY

On Date Three you will have the opportunity to work on your communication skills. Your relationship will only be as intimate as the conversations you have with each other. Words can help to build a deeper relationship, or they can damage it. Understanding three patterns of communication—chatting, confronting, and connecting—will help you choose more helpful patterns for the future. Chatting refers to surface conversations. The confronting pattern is the attacking style of communication. With the connecting pattern of communication you can deepen your relationship, become intimate, close companions, and even resolve differences. A simple grid (feelings formula) will help you share your deepest feelings without confronting your partner or defending yourself. Date Three will help you begin to develop the habit of using the connecting pattern of communication. It takes determination and practice, but you will be rewarded with a deeper, more meaningful relationship.

POST-DATE APPLICATION

- Keep looking for ways to compliment each other between now and the next date.
- Try to identify when you get into the confronting pattern of communication and stop before it escalates.
- See how much you can use the connecting pattern.
- Practice using the feelings formula.

> *Bonus date: Take ballroom or line dancing lessons, learn a new sport, or go canoeing together.*

Date Three Exercise

PART 1: FAMILY TALK

What was the communication style in your family of origin? Check your response. Then compare your list with your partner's list.
In my family:

___We openly shared our feelings, both negative and positive.
___We were always polite and never said what we really thought—peace at any price.
___We were a family of great debaters—a meal without a debate was boring.
___We rarely talked about anything significant.
___Other

PART 2: SHARING FEELINGS

1. What are our favorite topics to talk about (things about which we usually agree and promote good interaction)?

2. What are our less favorite topics (things we tend to debate about)?

3. Make a list of "feelings" words that you would feel comfortable using with each other.

4. Take turns answering the following questions:

How do I feel when

- you express appreciation for something I did?

- you smile at me?

- you make a sacrifice for me?

- you reach out and touch me?

- you tell me you love me?

- you tell me you are proud of me?

Date Three Exercise

PART 1: FAMILY TALK

What was the communication style in your family of origin? Check your response. Then compare your list with your partner's list.

In my family:

___We openly shared our feelings, both negative and positive.

___We were always polite and never said what we really thought—peace at any price.

___We were a family of great debaters—a meal without a debate was boring.

___We rarely talked about anything significant.

___Other

PART 2: SHARING FEELINGS

1. What are our favorite topics to talk about (things about which we usually agree and promote good interaction)?

2. What are our less favorite topics (things we tend to debate about)?

3. Make a list of "feelings" words that you would feel comfortable using with each other.

4. Take turns answering the following questions:

How do I feel when

- you express appreciation for something I did?

- you smile at me?

- you make a sacrifice for me?

- you reach out and touch me?

- you tell me you love me?

- you tell me you are proud of me?

Date Four
Solving Problems as a Couple

Date Four is crafted to help you learn ways to resolve ho est conflict by working through problems together.

PRE-DATE PREPARATION

- Read chapter 4, "Solving Problems as a Couple."
- Complete the Date Four Exercise.
- Choose a location that will allow you to talk quietly—maybe a coffee shop or a library. Even your local zoo might be fun for this date.

DATE NIGHT TIPS

- Continue to look for new insights about each other. This exercise can open new opportunities for growth and intimacy in your relationship.
- Review the communication tips in the Dating Ground Rules on page 154 with your partner before you begin discussing the exercise.
- If conflicts arise in your conversations, write them down and save for later; don't try to deal with them on this date.

CHAPTER SUMMARY

How do you solve problems as a couple? Do you attack the problem, or do you attack each other? Most couples from time to time struggle to stay positive and resist attacking the other. Which animal do you identify most with? (pages 56–57). Do you withdraw like the turtle or attack like the skunk? How would you like to be able to respond when you are angry? We believe the key to resolving conflict isn't the issue you are arguing about. Instead, the key is developing a way to look at that issue from the same side. The hard part of solving problems as a couple is discussing the problem in a civil way, and you will learn how to do that on this date by using the Speaker/Listener Technique. Actually, many of the issues we argue about aren't solvable or don't actually need a resolution, but we do need to be able to talk about them and understand each other's perspective. Once feelings are expressed and understood, the issue is fully

181

discussed, and you've both agreed on what the issue is and that you want a solution, you can move on to resolving the issues with four simple steps. In most cases, if you are willing to pull together, attack the problem and not each other, and do the hard work of problem discussion and problem solving, you will find a workable solution.

POST-DATE APPLICATION

- Look for ways to work together as a team to attack a problem and not each other.
- Practice the Speaker/Listener Technique so you fully understand each other's feelings. Do this before moving to problem solving.
- For problem solving, remember to use the four steps. And have fun while brainstorming.
- If on the date you wrote down any areas of conflicts, you may want to schedule a time to discuss these using the Speaker/Listener Technique. If you still have difficulty with them, ask your pastor, mentor couple, or counselor to help you work through them.

Bonus date: Have a "blue road" date. See what you can discover in a fifty mile radius without going on roads you are familiar with.

Date Four Exercise

PART 1: YOU AND YOUR FRIENDS AT THE ZOO

Before your date, rate yourself. Then on your date compare your lists and rankings.

What animal do you identify with the most in handling conflict? Rank from the most often used (1) to least often used (6).

___ Turtle—The Withdrawer   ___ Chameleon—The Yielder

___ Skunk—The Attacker   ___ Owl—The Intellectualizer

___ Gorilla—The Winner   ___ Beaver—The Avoider

___ Other

PART 2: PRACTICE THE SPEAKER/LISTENER TECHNIQUE

Choose topics from Date Three under "less favorite topics" (the ones you tend to debate) and write them here:

1.

2.

3.

Compare your list of topics with your partner's list. Together choose one area (preferably the one that is the least emotional for both of you) that you think would be the easiest to talk about. Remember to use the feelings formula as you discuss this topic using the Speaker/Listener Technique.

NOTE: *If you get into a negative pattern and have difficulty at this point, skip to Part 4. Later you can choose a time to repeat Part 2 and tackle Part 3.*

PART 3: PRACTICE PROBLEM SOLVING

From Part 2, write out the chosen issue.

The issue we wish to resolve is

Now go through the following four steps:

Step 1: Define the problem.

Step 2: Identify who has the need.

Step 3: Brainstorm possible solutions.

Step 4: Select a plan of action.

A question to ponder: If after trying to solve the problem you still needed help, who would you most likely consult? Your pastor? Mentor? Friend? Counselor? Other?

PART 4: HAVE SOME FUN!

Enough work for one date! After all, dating is supposed to be fun. Visit your favorite ice-cream or yogurt shop and get your favorite dessert. Celebrate progress you have made in being able to talk about touchy subjects. And if during the rest of your date, you discover some touchy subjects, don't discuss them now. Instead affirm that you are in the process of developing a communication system that really works and you're learning how to solve problems as a couple.

Date Four Exercise

PART 1: YOU AND YOUR FRIENDS AT THE ZOO

Before your date, rate yourself. Then on your date compare your lists and rankings.

What animal do you identify with the most in handling conflict? Rank from the most often used (1) to least often used (6).

___ Turtle—The Withdrawer ___ Chameleon—The Yielder

___ Skunk—The Attacker ___ Owl—The Intellectualizer

___ Gorilla—The Winner ___ Beaver—The Avoider

___ Other

PART 2: PRACTICE THE SPEAKER/LISTENER TECHNIQUE

Choose topics from Date Three under "less favorite topics" (the ones you tend to debate) and write them here:

1.

2.

3.

Compare your list of topics with your partner's list. Together choose one area (preferably the one that is the least emotional for both of you) that you think would be the easiest to talk about. Remember to use the feelings formula as you discuss this topic using the Speaker/Listener Technique.

NOTE: *If you get into a negative pattern and have difficulty at this point, skip to Part 4. Later you can choose a time to repeat Part 2 and tackle Part 3.*

10 Great Dates Before You Say "I Do" (Zondervan).
© 2003 David and Claudia Arp, Curt and Natelle Brown. Illegal to copy.

PART 3: PRACTICE PROBLEM SOLVING

From Part 2, write out the chosen issue.

The issue we wish to resolve is

Now go through the following four steps:

Step 1: Define the problem.

Step 2: Identify who has the need.

Step 3: Brainstorm possible solutions.

Step 4: Select a plan of action.

A question to ponder: If after trying to solve the problem you still needed help, who would you most likely consult? Your pastor? Mentor? Friend? Counselor? Other?

PART 4: HAVE SOME FUN!

Enough work for one date! After all, dating is supposed to be fun. Visit your favorite ice-cream or yogurt shop and get your favorite dessert. Celebrate progress you have made in being able to talk about touchy subjects. And if during the rest of your date, you discover some touchy subjects, don't discuss them now. Instead affirm that you are in the process of developing a communication system that really works and you're learning how to solve problems as a couple.

Date Five

Managing Your Money

Date Five will help you to talk about your expectations and consider how you might want to handle your finances after marriage.

PRE-DATE PREPARATION

- Read chapter 5, "Managing Your Money."
- Fill out the Date Five Exercise.
- Choose a location that will allow you to talk. Allow plenty of time to talk about this important issue.

DATE NIGHT TIPS

- Discuss your exercise, one point at a time.
- Money is a difficult subject for many people to discuss. Be extra sensitive to your partner's feelings.
- Even on a tough topic such as money, you can still have fun talking about financial planning and your financial dreams.

CHAPTER SUMMARY

How to handle finances is a huge issue, and you may be greatly influenced by how your parents handled family finances. Also in the past many couples married in their early twenties, and most didn't have a financial identity until after marriage. Today, couples are marrying later and may have already established a financial identity. They often have jobs, savings, 401k accounts, credit cards (often with accompanying debt), and college loans—all in their individual names—and they are used to controlling and managing their own money. If you are marrying later in life or if this is a second marriage, you may be bringing valuable assets into the marriage. It's critical to talk about finances *before* marriage so you have a complete understanding of what each is bringing into the relationship. To help you do that, we offer four practical steps for managing your money: evaluate your present debt, define your financial goals, develop a workable financial plan, and manage and monitor your

187

money. By being proactive, you can overcome the odds of financial conflict by working together on your financial plan before you say "I do."

POST-DATE APPLICATION

- Track your spending for the next few weeks.
- Continue to discuss your thoughts and feelings about money with your partner.
- Think of ways to reduce credit card debt.
- Express interest in your partner's work.

> *Bonus date: Go grocery shopping with $20 and see how far you can stretch it!*

Date Five Exercise

PART 1: YOUR FINANCIAL PAST

1. How did your family manage money as you were growing up? (Check all that apply.)

_____ Pinched every penny
_____ Borrowed money
_____ Saved for a rainy day
_____ Spent money like it grew on trees
_____ Invested wisely
_____ Donated to good causes
_____ Other

2. What things would you do the same as your family?

3. What would you do differently?

PART 2: YOUR FINANCIAL FUTURE

1. Discuss the debt that each of you might be bringing into your marriage. Is the total amount of debt tolerable to both of you?

2. What are the major categories you need in a future financial plan? Do you agree?

3. How do you think you might want to manage your money?

   ___ One pot—joint account

   ___ Two pots—separate accounts

   ___ Three pots—joint and separate accounts

4. Do you feel comfortable with your own and your partner's spending habits? If not, what changes would make you feel more comfortable?

5. If you received $5,000 as a wedding present, what would you do with the money?

PART 3: BALANCING CAREERS

1. What are your personal career goals?

2. How will you handle future career decisions? For example, if one had the opportunity for a promotion that required relocation, travel, or extended time commitment, what sacrifices would you be willing to make to advance your partner's career?

Date Five Exercise

PART 1: YOUR FINANCIAL PAST

1. How did your family manage money as you were growing up? (Check all that apply.)

    _____ Pinched every penny
    _____ Borrowed money
    _____ Saved for a rainy day
    _____ Spent money like it grew on trees
    _____ Invested wisely
    _____ Donated to good causes
    _____ Other

2. What things would you do the same as your family?

3. What would you do differently?

PART 2: YOUR FINANCIAL FUTURE

1. Discuss the debt that each of you might be bringing into your marriage. Is the total amount of debt tolerable to both of you?

2. What are the major categories you need in a future financial plan? Do you agree?

3. How do you think you might want to manage your money?

    ___ One pot—joint account

    ___ Two pots—separate accounts

    ___ Three pots—joint and separate accounts

4. Do you feel comfortable with your own and your partner's spending habits? If not, what changes would make you feel more comfortable?

5. If you received $5,000 as a wedding present, what would you do with the money?

PART 3: BALANCING CAREERS

1. What are your personal career goals?

2. How will you handle future career decisions? For example, if one had the opportunity for a promotion that required relocation, travel, or extended time commitment, what sacrifices would you be willing to make to advance your partner's career?

Date Six

Leaving and Cleaving

Date Six will help you better understand your families of origin, your expectations for future involvement with your families and your friends, and how to build your own friendship after marriage.

PRE-DATE PREPARATION

- Read chapter 6, "Leaving and Cleaving."
- Review the Date Six Exercise.
- Choose a location that will allow you to talk. This might be a good date to combine with an activity you both like to do, such as hiking, golfing, going on a picnic, or playing tennis.

DATE NIGHT TIPS

- Discuss your exercise, one point at a time.
- Be sensitive as you talk about your families of origin.
- Enjoy thinking about ways you can have fun together.

CHAPTER SUMMARY

How much do you know about each other's growing-up years? Many times couples assume that they know each other quite well and expect no surprises, yet each brings habit patterns to the marriage that the other may not be aware of. We also bring different friendship circles. On this date we look at three important principles: leaving our family of origin, blending our friendships, and cleaving to each other. While we naturally think of physically leaving our parents' home, it's more than that—it's also an attitude of reprioritizing our allegiance from our parents to our partner. Our friends must also realize that our loved one is a higher priority. Do you have any couple friendships that you both enjoy? If not, how can you develop some? Cleaving to each other means becoming best friends and soul mates. It means being that one person the other can always count on, sharing life on the deepest, most intimate level. Fun is also important in a marriage relationship, so you will want to keep on doing fun things together.

POST-DATE APPLICATION

- Look for ways to make your loved one a higher priority.
- Be creative and continue to think of fun things to do together.

> *Bonus date: Try a new activity that neither of you has done before, like bowling, horseback riding, or water skiing.*

Date Six Exercise

PART 1: LEAVING YOUR FAMILY OF ORIGIN

1. Look over "Questions to Ask Before the Wedding" beginning on page 80. Choose three or four you want to discuss with your partner.

2. What do you want to repeat or not repeat from your family of origin?

3. How can you love and respect your family and at the same time "leave" them for your future spouse?

PART 2: BLENDING FRIENDSHIPS AND MARRIAGE

1. Which mutual friends do you both enjoy?

2. If you have few mutual friends, do you want to build some couple friendships? How do you plan to go about this?

3. How do you think your individual friendships will affect your relationship after you are married?

PART 3: CLEAVING TO EACH OTHER

1. What kinds of things do you enjoy doing together (hobbies, interests, and recreational activities)?

2. What kinds of things do you enjoy doing separately?

3. Make a list of things you would like to learn or pursue together.

Date Six Exercise

PART 1: LEAVING YOUR FAMILY OF ORIGIN

1. Look over "Questions to Ask Before the Wedding" beginning on page 80. Choose three or four you want to discuss with your partner.

2. What do you want to repeat or not repeat from your family of origin?

3. How can you love and respect your family and at the same time "leave" them for your future spouse?

PART 2: BLENDING FRIENDSHIPS AND MARRIAGE

1. Which mutual friends do you both enjoy?

2. If you have few mutual friends, do you want to build some couple friendships? How do you plan to go about this?

3. How do you think your individual friendships will affect your relationship after you are married?

PART 3: CLEAVING TO EACH OTHER

1. What kinds of things do you enjoy doing together (hobbies, interests, and recreational activities)?

2. What kinds of things do you enjoy doing separately?

3. Make a list of things you would like to learn or pursue together.

10 Great Dates Before You Say "I Do" (Zondervan).
© 2003 David and Claudia Arp, Curt and Natelle Brown. Illegal to copy.

Date Seven

Celebrating Intimacy, Love, and Romance

This date will help you define what intimacy, love, and romance mean to you. You will have the opportunity to talk about the facets of a love life and how to get your differing desires and expectations in sync.

PRE-DATE PREPARATION

- Read chapter 7, "Celebrating Intimacy, Love, and Romance."
- Review the Date Seven Exercise.
- Choose a romantic restaurant or café where you can talk privately.

DATE NIGHT TIPS

- While this date is popular and fun, discussing these topics is tough for some people. Be sensitive to the other. Open up to your partner and share your feelings.
- You may want to review the communication skills in Date Three (page 43) and how to express feelings.
- Think of ways to make this date romantic—holding hands, going for a stroll in the moonlight, or walking in the rain.

CHAPTER SUMMARY

In a national survey, couples were asked what they considered to be the best aspects of their love life. While the responses varied, several themes emerged for a truly healthy love life: trust, mutuality, honesty, intimacy, affection, and sex. Trust is a basic component of any friendship and is essential in a romantic relationship. Having a mutual relationship involves a decision to choose each other above all others and to make your relationship a priority. Honesty is the ability to relate your true feelings. Are you willing to share your true feelings? Intimacy is the intangible quality of unity, understanding, and synergy that can move a relationship to the deep level as soul mates and lovers. Couples who experience a high level of intimacy often laugh a little more, are more affectionate, and are more likely to feel understood, accepted, and loved.

Affection is giving joy and comfort to each other through a touch, hug, kiss, or wink across the room. The culmination of a great love life is sex. In the beginning, God created sexuality, and his plan is that you experience a star-studded love life throughout the different seasons of your marriage. In each season you will have to work at staying lovers.

POST-DATE APPLICATION

- Look for ways to express affection to your partner.
- Encourage your loved one daily.
- Demonstrate your devotion to your partner (see page 105 for practical suggestions).

> *Bonus date: Plan your ultimate dream honeymoon or vacation over the Internet, but don't book it!*

Date Seven Exercise

PART 1: FACETS OF A STAR-STUDDED LOVE LIFE

Consider the following six facets. On a scale of 1 to 5 (1 being not so important and 5 being very important) rank each as to how important each facet is to you. Now rank them as you think your partner would rank them. Compare your lists and discuss.

___ ___ Trust—Feeling safe with each other

___ ___ Mutuality—Freely choosing to love each other

___ ___ Honesty—Openly communicating your true feelings

___ ___ Intimacy—Being soul mates and feeling close

___ ___ Affection—Giving joy and comfort to each other

___ ___ Sex—Joining together physically and loving each other

PART 2: ROMANCE AND INTIMACY

1. What would be your top three romantic moments together?

    •

    •

    •

2. What is your idea of the best expressions of love?

PART 3: EXPECTATIONS

1. When I think of intimacy and closeness,

2. My idea of romance is

PART 4: HONEYMOON PLANS (IF APPLICABLE)

In what ways will your honeymoon plans fulfill your definition of romance and intimacy?

Date Seven Exercise

PART 1: FACETS OF A STAR-STUDDED LOVE LIFE

Consider the following six facets. On a scale of 1 to 5 (1 being not so important and 5 being very important) rank each as to how important each facet is to you. Now rank them as you think your partner would rank them. Compare your lists and discuss.

___ ___ Trust—Feeling safe with each other

___ ___ Mutuality—Freely choosing to love each other

___ ___ Honesty—Openly communicating your true feelings

___ ___ Intimacy—Being soul mates and feeling close

___ ___ Affection—Giving joy and comfort to each other

___ ___ Sex—Joining together physically and loving each other

PART 2: ROMANCE AND INTIMACY

1. What would be your top three romantic moments together?

   •

   •

   •

2. What is your idea of the best expressions of love?

PART 3: EXPECTATIONS

1. When I think of intimacy and closeness,

2. My idea of romance is

PART 4: HONEYMOON PLANS (IF APPLICABLE)

In what ways will your honeymoon plans fulfill your definition of romance and intimacy?

Date Eight

Realizing Roles and Planning for Family

This date will help you talk candidly about your expectations concerning roles in marriage, how you want to divide and share chores and life tasks, and your expectations concerning family planning.

PRE-DATE PREPARATION

- Read chapter 8, "Realizing Roles and Planning for Family."
- Review the Date Eight Exercise.
- Choose a location where you can talk. You might want to go out for dinner so neither of you will have to cook or clean the kitchen.

DATE NIGHT TIPS

- This date doesn't have to be work. Concentrate on finding balance.
- In discussing your roles, think about your abilities.
- When talking about division of responsibilities, remember you are a team.
- Begin thinking about how children will impact your relationship.

CHAPTER SUMMARY

What happens along the way that changes pre-marriage expectations about roles and responsibilities to the reality that one ends up with more than half the work? One answer is lack of communication and lack of having a plan. Many times, couples don't talk about roles and responsibilities before marriage. Marital research reveals that happier couples share responsibilities, so how can you make sure you will equally share the load? You can begin by assessing your responsibilities—or those you plan to assume when you are married. Who does what is not as important as the philosophy of sharing the load together.

Another major topic for this date is talking about your future hopes and dreams concerning children. While having a baby is exciting, marriage satisfaction dips for most couples when they become parents. Because of the time pressures children bring, couples need to be reminded to keep fun and friendship in their marriage. Children can enrich your marriage, and your marriage can enrich your children. Now is the time to consider your future roles and to talk about family planning.

POST-DATE APPLICATION

- Think of things you could do around the house to help your partner.
- Have the mind-set that you are going to work together. It can make a big difference in your attitude and outlook in life.

> *Bonus date: Prepare a meal together, do some other household or lawn project together, or do nursery duty together at church.*

Date Eight Exercise

PART 1: HIS AND HERS HOUSEHOLD TASKS

What things do you assume you will do around the house? What things do you assume your partner will do around the house? Mark "M" for Male, "F" for Female, "B" for Both. (You may also want to indicate who did what in your family of origin.)

____Shopping ____Vacuuming

____Preparing for meals ____Taking out garbage

____Making beds ____Cleaning out closets

____Caring for the lawn ____Paying the bills

____Maintaining cars ____Balancing the checkbook

____Cleaning bathrooms ____Preparing tax returns

____Doing laundry ____Doing household repairs

____Ironing ____Scheduling appointments

____Dusting ____Keeping financial records

____Buying groceries ____Returning DVDs and videos

____Caring for pets ____Other

After you both have marked your lists, compare and discuss them. What will the two of you do to negotiate and compromise to share responsibilities?

PART 2: PLANNING FOR FAMILY

1. Do you both want to have children? How many? When?

2. If you were unable to have children, would you consider adoption?

3. How will role responsibilities change when you become parents?

4. How did your parents share parenting responsibilities?

5. What is your attitude toward working parents? Should one partner stay at home to raise the children?

6. If either of you are bringing children into the marriage, how will they affect your relationship?

Date Eight Exercise

PART 1: HIS AND HERS HOUSEHOLD TASKS

What things do you assume you will do around the house? What things do you assume your partner will do around the house? Mark "M" for Male, "F" for Female, "B" for Both. (You may also want to indicate who did what in your family of origin.)

____Shopping   ____Vacuuming

____Preparing for meals   ____Taking out garbage

____Making beds   ____Cleaning out closets

____Caring for the lawn   ____Paying the bills

____Maintaining cars   ____Balancing the checkbook

____Cleaning bathrooms   ____Preparing tax returns

____Doing laundry   ____Doing household repairs

____Ironing   ____Scheduling appointments

____Dusting   ____Keeping financial records

____Buying groceries   ____Returning DVDs and videos

____Caring for pets   ____Other

After you both have marked your lists, compare and discuss them. What will the two of you do to negotiate and compromise to share responsibilities?

10 Great Dates Before You Say "I Do" (Zondervan).
© 2003 David and Claudia Arp, Curt and Natelle Brown. Illegal to copy.

PART 2: PLANNING FOR FAMILY

1. Do you both want to have children? How many? When?

2. If you were unable to have children, would you consider adoption?

3. How will role responsibilities change when you become parents?

4. How did your parents share parenting responsibilities?

5. What is your attitude toward working parents? Should one partner stay at home to raise the children?

6. If either of you are bringing children into the marriage, how will they affect your relationship?

Date Nine

Developing Spiritual Intimacy

The purpose of this date is to share together where you are on your spiritual quest and to look at ways to develop spiritual intimacy.

PRE-DATE PREPARATION

- Read chapter 9, "Developing Spiritual Intimacy."
- Preview the Date Nine Exercise.
- Choose a location where you can quietly reflect together. You might want to go to a chapel.

DATE NIGHT TIPS

- If you are at different places on your spiritual journey, be sensitive to one another.
- Talk about what you have in common.
- This is an opportunity to share your inner feelings. It is not a time to try to change your partner.

CHAPTER SUMMARY

Now, as you are considering marriage, is a great time to also consider the role you want spirituality to play in your lives together. What spiritual beliefs are you bringing into your marriage? Do you both have a personal relationship with Christ? What were the religious practices and spiritual beliefs of your family of origin? Did you grow up in a Christian home? How important is the spiritual dimension of life to you as an adult? Are prayer, Bible study, and meditation important parts of your life? What about participation in a faith community and fellowship with other believers? Do you both participate in religious activities? If you are from different spiritual backgrounds, how do you plan to handle that after marriage? On this date you will want to talk about your own spiritual values and beliefs and find the common bonds between you as a couple. Spiritual intimacy manifests itself in unconditional love and acceptance, forgiveness, prayer, and service to others.

POST-DATE APPLICATION

- Together write a list of your shared core beliefs.
- Commit to growing together spiritually.
- Read a book together on a topic related to spiritual growth.
- Think about joining a fellowship group or couples Bible study.

Bonus date: Choose a service project to do together, such as Habitat for Humanity, help with a church youth group, or run errands for an elderly person.

Date Nine Exercise

PART 1: TAKING A SPIRITUAL INTIMACY CHECK-UP

Consider the following aspects of spirituality. On a scale of 1 to 5 (1 being not so important and 5 being very important) rate each as to how important each facet is to you. Now rate them as you think your partner would rate them. Compare your lists and discuss.

___ ___ Attending church and worshiping together

___ ___ Participating in church activities (Bible studies, fellowships, growth groups)

___ ___ Having a personal faith in God

___ ___ Giving to the church and other charities

___ ___ Forgiving each other

___ ___ Accepting each other unconditionally

___ ___ Celebrating religious holidays

___ ___ Reading the Bible together

___ ___ Having devotions together

___ ___ Praying together

___ ___ Serving others together

___ ___ Other

PART 2: THEN AND NOW

1. Describe the spiritual atmosphere in your home as you were growing up.

2. Where are you on your spiritual journey?

3. What are your core beliefs?

4. What core beliefs do you share?

5. What could you do to serve others?

Date Nine Exercise

PART 1: TAKING A SPIRITUAL INTIMACY CHECK-UP

Consider the following aspects of spirituality. On a scale of 1 to 5 (1 being not so important and 5 being very important) rate each as to how important each facet is to you. Now rate them as you think your partner would rate them. Compare your lists and discuss.

___ ___ Attending church and worshiping together

___ ___ Participating in church activities (Bible studies, fellowships, growth groups)

___ ___ Having a personal faith in God

___ ___ Giving to the church and other charities

___ ___ Forgiving each other

___ ___ Accepting each other unconditionally

___ ___ Celebrating religious holidays

___ ___ Reading the Bible together

___ ___ Having devotions together

___ ___ Praying together

___ ___ Serving others together

___ ___ Other

PART 2: THEN AND NOW

1. Describe the spiritual atmosphere in your home as you were growing up.

2. Where are you on your spiritual journey?

3. What are your core beliefs?

4. What core beliefs do you share?

5. What could you do to serve others?

Date Ten

Choosing an Intentional Marriage

This date will help you consider what marriage involvement style will work best for you and will encourage you to set marriage goals to help you turn your desires and dreams for your marriage into reality.

PRE-DATE APPLICATION

- Read chapter 10, "Choosing an Intentional Marriage."
- Fill out the Date Ten Exercise.
- Choose a location where you can have access to a table. Your local library or bookstore with a coffee shop might be a fun place for this date.

DATE NIGHT TIPS

- Take your time; don't race through this date. You are talking about the rest of your lives.
- Set at least one goal that you both want to achieve, but don't be overambitious. It's better to reach one goal than to have ten that you don't reach.

CHAPTER SUMMARY

Marriage is a big choice, and we hope we have helped you understand each other better so you can make a wise choice as you consider marriage. Can you now answer the big questions, "Can I live with this other person for a lifetime?" "Do we have the skills and attitudes we need to build a successful marriage?" Or, if you are seriously dating, "Am I ready to move forward to a deeper level of commitment?" The real value of reexamining and reconfirming your decision to marry is when you do marry, you will marry with confidence. You can say with assurance, "Yes, I have chosen wisely." So if you have any lingering concerns, now is the time to discuss them. Also, we encourage you to find a mentor couple. Then spend some time talking about what marriage involvement style will work for you. We hope this date will help you set realistic goals for your marriage. Few couples ever take the time to set specific objectives for their marriages, much less make a plan to accomplish them. Basically, a marriage goal is a target toward which you agree to work. As you devise an action plan, use three simple words to guide you: What? How? When? Answer these questions and you're on your way to an intentional marriage!

POST-DATE APPLICATION

- Follow the plan you have just made.
- Keep looking for the positive and complimenting each other (by now, this should be a habit).
- Continue the habit of dating (you may want to repeat these ten dates).
- Together make a list of future dates you would like to have.
- Remember that your relationship will remain alive and healthy as you nurture it.

> *Bonus date: Have a date to plan fun dates for the next few weeks!*

Date Ten

PART 1: CHOOSE YOUR MARRIAGE INVOLVEMENT STYLE

Degrees of Involvement in Marriage

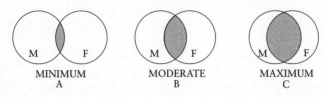

| MINIMUM | MODERATE | MAXIMUM |
| A | B | C |

1. What would be the ideal involvement style for your marriage?

2. What do you think will be realistic as you start your marriage?

PART 2: CHOOSE A MENTOR

If you don't already have a mentor couple, make a list of older couples you could ask to be mentors to you. You may want to check with your church to see if a mentoring program is already in place.

PART 3: MAKE TIME FOR EACH OTHER

Talk through the following four steps (refer to page 133):

1. Make a commitment.

2. Analyze your present time constraints.

3. Set apart time for your relationship.

4. Guard your time.

PART 4: SETTING GOALS FOR YOUR MARRIAGE

What goals would you like to set for your upcoming marriage?

Answer these three questions:

1. What? (Choose one goal.)

2. How? (Consider what steps you will need to take to help accomplish your goal.)

3. When? (Note it in your Palm Pilot or calendar!)

10 Great Dates Before You Say "I Do" (Zondervan).
© 2003 David and Claudia Arp, Curt and Natelle Brown. Illegal to copy.

Date Ten

PART 1: CHOOSE YOUR MARRIAGE INVOLVEMENT STYLE

Degrees of Involvement in Marriage

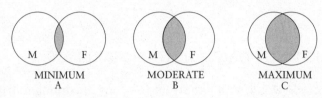

1. What would be the ideal involvement style for your marriage?

2. What do you think will be realistic as you start your marriage?

PART 2: CHOOSE A MENTOR

If you don't already have a mentor couple, make a list of older couples you could ask to be mentors to you. You may want to check with your church to see if a mentoring program is already in place.

PART 3: MAKE TIME FOR EACH OTHER

Talk through the following four steps (refer to page 133):

    1. Make a commitment.

    2. Analyze your present time constraints.

3. Set apart time for your relationship.

4. Guard your time.

PART 4: SETTING GOALS FOR YOUR MARRIAGE

What goals would you like to set for your upcoming marriage?

Answer these three questions:

1. What? (Choose one goal.)

2. How? (Consider what steps you will need to take to help accomplish your goal.)

3. When? (Note it in your Palm Pilot or calendar!)

Share Your Thoughts

With the Author: Your comments will be forwarded to the author when you send them to *zauthor@zondervan.com*.

With Zondervan: Submit your review of this book by writing to *zreview@zondervan.com*.

Free Online Resources at

www.zondervan.com

Zondervan AuthorTracker: Be notified whenever your favorite authors publish new books, go on tour, or post an update about what's happening in their lives.

Daily Bible Verses and Devotions: Enrich your life with daily Bible verses or devotions that help you start every morning focused on God.

Free Email Publications: Sign up for newsletters on fiction, Christian living, church ministry, parenting, and more.

Zondervan Bible Search: Find and compare Bible passages in a variety of translations at www.zondervanbiblesearch.com.

Other Benefits: Register yourself to receive online benefits like coupons and special offers, or to participate in research.